Hearts and Minds Uplifted

◆

The Power of Falun Dafa

Clearwisdom Editors

Published by :

Taiwan
BROAD PRESS INTERNATIONAL CO., LTD.
10F.-2, No.626, Sec. 4, Bade Rd., Songshan District,
Taipei City 105, Taiwan (R.O.C.)
Telephone : 02-27690599
Fax : 02-27160761

ISBN : 1-932674-34-9

First printed July, 2006
Revised December, 2006

Printed in Taiwan

Hearts and Minds Uplifted

◆

The Power of Falun Dafa

Table of Contents

Introduction

Although Falun Gong (also known as Falun Dafa) is deeply rooted in ancient Chinese culture, it was first introduced to the public in 1992 by Mr. Li Hongzhi, the practice's founder and teacher. Now, over 100 million people worldwide perform the simple, graceful exercises on a daily basis while striving to conduct themselves according to Falun Dafa's fundamental guiding principles: Truthfulness, Compassion, and Forbearance.

The vast majority of people who take up the practice experience significant improvements in many aspects of their lives. A previously published collection of short articles, *Life and Hope Renewed--The Healing Power of Falun Dafa*, described the profound health benefits of Falun Dafa. This companion volume focuses on another important aspect of people's lives: the tremendous personal growth that can be achieved by cultivating one's character through practicing Falun Gong.

The Origins of Falun Dafa

From 1992 to 1994, Mr. Li Hongzhi gave over 50 lecture series on the practice, typically consisting of a two-hour class every day for nine days. During the classes, generally one and a half hours were used to lecture on the principles of Falun Dafa, and the last half hour was used to teach the exercises. By the end of a lecture series, attendees would have received the essential teachings and learned all of the exercises.

In December 1994, the main text of Falun Dafa, *Zhuan Falun*, was published, and at this time the lecture series came to an end. The book provided newcomers who had not attended the lecture series the opportunity to learn the practice on their own. Veteran practitioners benefited as well, as this book became the cornerstone text for continuous improvement, providing practitioners with guidance at every stage of their cultivation.

Because of its tremendous power to improve health and elevate character, Falun Dafa stood out from the myriad of other qigong systems being taught and practiced in China at that time. Before July 1999, by early dawn, almost every Chinese park would be brimming with people practicing the exercises, which were always taught free of charge by volunteers in each city. Spread primarily by word of mouth, Falun Dafa grew very quickly. The practitioners came from different geographic regions and spanned all ages, social strata and walks of life. Many government agencies and mainstream media acknowledged and supported Falun Dafa.

Cultivation Practice

Falun Dafa is a cultivation practice for elevating the mind and enhancing physical health. Although the concept of "cultivation" may not be familiar to many Westerners, looking through the list of definitions of "cultivate" in the dictionary, we do find that it relates to "growth, development, improvement, and refinement of something," in this case, a person, through "education, training, labor, and attention." But this does not tell the whole story.

In China, there is a rich tradition of cultivation. The term in Chinese is *xiu lian*. *Xiu* means to "repair" or "fix." *Lian* means to "smelt" or "refine," and written in Chinese, this character looks similar to and has the same pronunciation as the term "to practice [exercises]." This is only a direct translation of the characters that make up the term.

To get a more complete understanding of the concept of cultivation, we can look to China's history. Around 2,500 years ago, the sage Lao Zi appeared in China. Around the same time, Shakyamuni appeared in India. Lao Zi wrote the book *Dao De Jing*, which was how most people learned about what he called the "Dao" or the "Way." Shakyamuni spread Buddhism in India for 49 years, which then made its way to China. These two schools then formed the basis for many spiritual practices in China.

Religions are also considered forms of cultivation. For example, there is the religion of Buddhism, which has temples, monks and nuns, rituals, and many other formalities of a religion, and there are many different denominations of Buddhism. The cultivation way of the Buddha school does not end there though, as there are many practices from this school that are not considered part of the Buddhist religion. Often these practices are comprised of simply a teacher and students, but there are no religious formalities or places of worship. These are also considered cultivation ways. The same is true for the Daoist school. There is the religion of Daoism, but there are also many Daoist practices that are not religions. So in China, it is not considered necessary to be a member of a religion in order to achieve the goal of elevating one's spiritual level—but one does need a cultivation practice. Here in the West, since we don't really have the concept of cultivation, anything spiritual or that has to do with transcending the human world has traditionally fallen under the concept of religion.

Falun Dafa is such a cultivation way, encompassing the essence of all other cultivation ways in the form of its guiding principles, Truthfulness, Compassion, and Forbearance. Indeed, regardless of their religious affiliation or spiritual beliefs, people can universally identify with these three core principles of Falun Dafa.

The Practice of Falun Dafa

Many of the essential truths of Falun Dafa were taught in private for thousands of years. It was common in China's history to teach this way, as these timeless principles were often passed from a teacher to a single student. In the 1960's and 1970's, many qigong practices were introduced to the public. At that time, mostly just exercises and some basic principles were taught, and by doing these qigong exercises, people were able to improve their health.

Since Falun Dafa is a cultivation practice for both the mind and body, a practitioner not only does the exercises to transform the energy of his body for increased health, but also strives to elevate his character by following the principles of Truthfulness, Compassion and Forbearance.

The five exercises themselves are easy to learn and practice. Mr. Li Hongzhi gives explanations of each of the exercises in *The Great Consummation Way of Falun Dafa*, portions of which are quoted below:

The first exercise is called "Buddha Showing a Thousand Hands."

"At the core of Buddha Showing a Thousand Hands is stretching of the body. This stretching unblocks areas where energy is congested, stimulates the energy within the body and under the skin so that it circulates vigorously, and automatically absorbs a great amount of energy from the universe. This enables all of the meridians in a practitioner's body to open at the beginning. When one performs this exercise, the body will have a special feeling of warmth and of the existence of a strong energy field. This is caused by the stretching and opening of all meridians throughout the body."

The second exercise is called "The Falun Standing Stance."

"Falun Standing Stance is a tranquil standing meditation composed of four wheel-holding positions. Frequent performance of Falun Standing Stance will facilitate the complete opening of the entire body. It is a comprehensive means of cultivation practice that enhances wisdom, increases strength, raises one's level, and strengthens divine powers. The movements are simple, but much can be achieved through the exercise. Beginners' arms may feel heavy and painful. After doing the exercises, the whole body will immediately feel relaxed, without feeling the kind of fatigue that comes from working."

The third exercise is called "Penetrating the Two Cosmic Extremes."

"Penetrating the Two Cosmic Extremes channels the cosmos' energy and mixes it with the energy inside one's body. A great amount of energy is expelled and taken in during this exercise, enabling a practitioner to purify his or her body in a very short time. At the same time, the exercise opens the meridians on top of the head and unblocks the passages underneath the feet."

The fourth exercise is called "The Great Heavenly Circuit."

"Falun Heavenly Circuit enables the energy of the human body to circulate over large areas—that is, not just in one or several meridians, but from the entire yin side to the entire yang side of the body, back and forth continuously. This exercise is far beyond the usual methods of opening the meridians or the Great and Small Heavenly Circuits. Falun Heavenly Circuit is an intermediate-level cultivation method. With the previous three exercises as a base, the meridians of the entire body (including the Great Heavenly Circuit) can be quickly opened through performing this exercise."

The fifth exercise is called "Strengthening Divine Powers."

"Strengthening Divine Powers is a tranquil cultivation exercise. It's a multi-purpose exercise that strengthens divine powers (including supernormal abilities) and gong potency by turning the Falun using Buddha hand signs. This exercise is above the intermediate level and was originally a secret exercise. Performing this exercise requires sitting with both legs crossed. Single-leg crossing is acceptable at the initial stage if double-leg crossing cannot be done."

Cultivation of Character

Although Falun Dafa has physical exercises, they are supplementary to the cultivation of one's character, or *xinxing* (see glossary). In general, this is done by studying *Zhuan Falun*, the core text containing the teachings of Falun Dafa, and by living according to the principles of Truthfulness, Compassion and Forbearance. The importance placed on the elevation of character separates Falun Dafa from most other qigong practices popularized in China over the past several decades, as other practices focus primarily on physical exercises for health and fitness.

The meaning of the term "character," as it is used in the practice of Falun Gong, is somewhat broader than its dictionary definition. In *Zhuan Falun*, Master Li describes it this way:

> "So what is character? Character includes virtue (which is a type of matter), it includes enduring, it includes awakening to things, it includes giving up things—giving up all the desires and all the attachments that are found in an ordinary person—and you also have to endure hardship, to name just a few things. So it includes a lot of different things. You need to improve every aspect of your character, and only when you do that will you really improve."

As a practitioner cultivates character, he or she treats everything that happens in daily life as a test and an opportunity to improve. For example, if someone berates a practitioner, he or she would take this as an opportunity to put Truthfulness, Compassion and Forbearance into practice. Rather than getting upset and responding in kind, perhaps the practitioner would understand that it would be best to just let it go, or calmly and kindly explain the situation that brought about the conflict. There are no formulas providing specific ways to act in every situation, but by reading *Zhuan Falun*, practitioners gain their own understanding of how to cultivate character and how to take these tribulations that all of us meet in our lives as opportunities to improve.

Practitioners find that as they cultivate, they are frequently gaining new understandings of how to live according to Truthfulness, Compassion and Forbearance. Perhaps in the beginning of cultivation, a practitioner might respond one way when insulted, but after cultivating for a while and gaining a better understanding of the principles, he might treat the same situation quite differently.

Another aspect of cultivating character that is frequently mentioned in this book involves "letting go of attachments." It is important to note that this is not the same concept as striving to become detached from life or one's problems. On the contrary, it's a process of facing up to one's shortcomings and life's difficulties and rising above them. In the context of cultivation practice, "letting go of attachments" refers to gradually giving up notions, behaviors, and thought patterns that prevent a person from fully assimilating to Truthfulness, Compassion, and Forbearance.

The relationship between mental and physical health is extremely important. By cultivating character, practitioners are also directly and positively affecting their physical health. This is thought to be one reason why the practice of Falun Dafa has such outstanding results in healing illnesses.

Scientific Findings

The precise way in which the practice of Falun Dafa works to heal illness is not fully understood by modern science, but its effects can be measured through scientific study.

A Chinese government census taken in 1998 indicated that 70 to 100 million people were practicing Falun Dafa in China alone. This made Falun Dafa by far the most popular qigong practice in China's history. Many practitioners testified from their personal experience that Falun Dafa had powerful healing properties. In 1998, the first major health survey was conducted on Falun Dafa practitioners in Beijing.

According to the survey, out of 12,731 participants, 93.4% initially had conditions of illness and 49.8% had suffered from at least three diseases before they began practicing Falun Dafa. Through learning and practicing Falun Dafa, the practitioners' health improved to varying degrees, with 58.5% reporting complete recovery. Comparing practitioners' health before and after practicing Falun Dafa, 80.3% of the participants reported improvements. Among these people, the percentage of people reporting that they felt "very energetic" increased from 3.5 before practicing to 55.3 after practicing. These numbers demonstrate that Falun Dafa is remarkably effective in curing illness, increasing energy, and improving one's overall sense of well-being. Being healthy includes having both a healthy body and a healthy mind. The survey demonstrated that 12,287 people, or 96.5% of the participants, felt healthier psychologically after practicing Falun Dafa.

The Beijing survey indicated that the number of people practicing Falun Dafa increased every year, with the growth rate also becoming more rapid. The fact that Falun Dafa attracted such a great number of practitioners in such a short time provides further evidence that Falun Dafa is indeed effective in healing illness and improving health.

According to the survey, Falun Dafa practitioners saved 3,270 *yuan* in medical expenses per person per year for the nation. Multiplying this figure by the millions of people practicing, one can easily see that Falun Dafa saved China a tremendous amount of money in medical costs and resources. This is one of the reasons why Falun Dafa has been widely regarded as being beneficial, not just for individuals, but also for society as a whole.

A survey was also conducted in Taiwan. Out of 1,182 participants, 72% of Falun Dafa practitioners used only one health insurance card, which allows the recipient 6 visits to health care providers, per year, a reduction in usage of almost 50% compared to the general population. The report also pointed out that Falun Dafa has a remarkable effect on eliminating unhealthy habits and addictions. The study showed an 81% success rate for quitting smoking, 77% for abstaining from alcohol, and 85% for quitting gambling.

To learn more about Falun Dafa's profound healing powers, please read *Life and Hope Renewed--The Healing Power of Falun Dafa.*

The Persecution in China: "Ruin their reputations, bankrupt them financially, and destroy them physically."

Because of the great benefits offered by the practice of Falun Dafa, it quickly became the most popular form of qigong in China, with the number of practitioners exceeding the total membership of the Communist Party. Its immense popularity drew the attention of Jiang Zemin, then Chairman, Communist Party General Secretary, and Head of the Military Commission in China. As the powerful head of the Communist Party, which has stamped out any diversity of thought since its inception, Jiang and others in the Party leadership ordered the police to curtail Falun Dafa activities and the state-run media to reverse course and publish defamatory stories about Falun Dafa.

In response to a set of such articles, a group of practitioners went to the magazine agency in the city of Tianjin to clarify some facts about Falun Dafa, hoping to resolve any misunderstandings that may have taken place. To their surprise, their peaceful discussions were interrupted when over 300 riot police descended upon them, physically assaulting them and arresting 45 of them. When questioned, the Tianjin authorities directed the practitioners to take their appeal to Beijing, stating that the arrests were made at the directive of the Central Government.

On April 25, 1999, about 10,000 Falun Dafa practitioners went to the State Council's Appeals Bureau near Zhongnanhai to lodge an appeal. Then-Premier Zhu Rongji met with these practitioners and at the end of the day ordered the Tianjin police to release the wrongfully arrested practitioners and repeated the government's policy of not interfering with people's freedom to practice.

Although the incident was peacefully resolved, Jiang Zemin saw this as an opportunity to eliminate a perceived threat. On July 20, 1999, Jiang launched the full-blown persecution with mass arrests, beatings, and unlawful detention of tens of thousands of Falun Dafa practitioners. The police burned Falun Dafa books and ransacked practitioners' homes, and the media saturated the country with propaganda to defame Falun Dafa. Later, when the suppression of Falun Gong proved more difficult than anticipated, Jiang issued the infamous directive which created the genocidal nature of this persecution: "Ruin their reputations, bankrupt them financially, and destroy them physically."

After seven years of intense, nationwide persecution, millions of practitioners have been arrested, detained, or sent to forced labor camps without trial. Thousands have been sent to mental hospitals to be injected with psychotropic drugs, and women have been sexually abused in police custody. Some have even been forced to have abortions against their will. And recently, even more appalling atrocities have been revealed: China's vast network of labor camps, detention centers, and secret concentration camps are being used to facilitate the harvesting of organs from living Falun Gong practitioners, to be sold for profit in the transplant trade. The bodies are then cremated to destroy the evidence.

As of this writing, close to 3,000 practitioners are verified to have died in police custody, most as a result of torture, but when all of the Chinese Communist Party's dark secrets are revealed, the actual figure will almost certainly be shown to be much higher.

Outside of China, Falun Dafa has flourished throughout the rest of the world. The practice has spread to more than 70 countries, receiving more than 1100 awards and other forms of recognition from local governments and civic organizations. In the meantime, in spite of the brutality that the practitioners in China have been subjected to, there has not been a single case of retaliation or violence on the part of the practitioners. The last seven years stand as a powerful testament to the universal appeal of "Truthfulness, Compassion, Forbearance" and the firm resolve of the people that live according to these principles

Conclusion

In a very brief period of time, Falun Dafa and the teachings of Mr. Li Hongzhi have exerted a powerful and beneficial influence throughout the world. To further share the benefits of Falun Gong, we have published this volume of short articles by people whose practice of Falun Dafa uplifted their hearts and minds and gave them a renewed life of spiritual and physical well-being.

Millions of people around the world have improved their physical health and elevated their character through practicing Falun Dafa, and the stories presented here represent only a tiny fraction of those who have benefited. Many people begin to experience positive changes simply by reading *Zhuan Falun*, while others find improvements taking place gradually over a period of time in which they diligently practice the exercises and study the teachings. Practicing Falun Dafa for the sole purpose of healing one's physical illness is not encouraged, but many practitioners have experienced that when they let go of their attachments, elevate their hearts and minds, and conduct their lives according to "Truthfulness, Compassion, and Forbearance," problems that seem insurmountable through conventional means very often miraculously disappear.

The Enormous Power of Dafa

By Peter Jauhal, U.K.

I came across Falun Gong on the Internet in March 1996. I downloaded the materials and started reading them with my wife. We were both very impressed by the philosophy, and the exercises made an immediate impact. Everything made sense to us and there was nothing that we could not accept. We both had an immense feeling of happiness because we had finally found what we had been looking for.

At that time there were no classes in the UK, but one week later I went to Sweden to attend a Falun Gong conference. I spent six days in Sweden and met many practitioners. I was very impressed by the friendliness and kindness of the practitioners and enjoyed my time there enormously. At the end of the six days, I knew that Falun Gong was something that was very good and also that it was something that I could practice well.

Since that time I have changed in every way. In the following pages I will explain some of the changes that I have noticed.

At work my performance has increased enormously. I am a management consultant and my job involves advising companies on how to manage their employees. Before practicing Falun Gong I was determined to reach the top of my company as quickly as possible. When I did not receive a promotion that I was expecting I would become very upset. Since practicing Falun Gong I have not fretted about promotions at all. I try to do the best for my clients and really listen to what they want to achieve, without worrying about the profit that I will make on the project. If someone else can help the client more than I can, I will tell the client to work with that person rather than try to get the project for myself. In fact I price my projects very reasonably now because I do not want to treat any client unfairly. In the last two years I have been promoted twice and I am selling four times as much business for my company than I did before. I am sure this would not have happened if I had not practiced Falun Gong.

Also at work, Falun Gong has helped me to cope with the stress in my job. In my work, a mistake can cost my company many hundreds of thousands of pounds. Before I began practicing Falun Gong there were several occasions when I would not be able to sleep at night because I would worry about my work. Since I have been practicing Falun Gong I have slept very soundly even though the pressure in my job has increased. This is because I no longer have an unhealthy attachment to my job or my position in the company. I always try to do the best that I can. If I make a mistake, I correct it as quickly as possible and carry on. I never try to hide my mistakes anymore.

In my home life I have also changed. Before practicing Falun Gong I was attached to having the best of everything. I was very materialistic and very competitive. I was attached to having the latest electronic gadgets, the best car, house, vacation, clothes, food, etc. Today I am different. I only buy things that are essential and I have given away many of the things that I had bought before. I have paid off all of the money that I owed. I have tried to simplify my life as much as I can.

Since practicing Falun Gong, I have noticed that I have much more energy. Before, I would need to sleep at least 8 hours every night. Now I sleep between 4 and 5 hours every night and do not feel tired at all. I use the extra time to do other things now.

My personality has also changed. Before practicing Falun Gong I was always seeking the best way to achieve my personal goals in every situation. Now I always try to think of how to best help the people around me. For example, I often spend my spare time volunteering to give Falun Gong classes so that others can benefit from this, too. Before practicing Falun Gong I could never have imagined that I would spend much time on an activity without any financial reward.

One test that I have at the moment is to treat all the people that I meet the same. At work and in my private life there are some people that I meet that I instantly like and others that I have a negative view of. I do not say this to them but I think it in my mind. I realize that this is the result of my attachments. I tend to like people who think the same way I do and dislike people who do not think the way I do. This means that I think my way of thinking is the best, which, of course, is an attachment. For example, a new person came to a Falun Gong class in London. She did not speak very nicely and was rude to the people around her and to me. I had the view that only "nice" people would become serious Falun Gong practitioners. I thought that this lady would not be able to do the exercises and would give up Falun Gong very quickly. I was surprised to see that she could do the exercises very well and for over one and a half hours on her first day, and that she later bought the book *Falun Gong*. This shows how incorrect it is for me to judge people based on my own conceptions.

In conclusion, I think that Falun Dafa is the most wonderful thing in my life. It has made me into a much better person and made my life so much simpler and happier. In the future I will try my best to improve further.

Thanks To Falun Gong, I Have Become Much More Considerate of Others—And I Look Younger, Too!

By Lin Yu-Hsia, Taiwan

Ever since I was a child, I have been very outgoing and active. My family nicknamed me "wild horse." I enjoyed sports and won many awards while representing my elementary and secondary schools in open tournaments. However, academically I fell far short. Nonetheless, the high marks I achieved by playing sports compensated for my poor performance in other subjects.

In order to relieve the financial situation at home, I followed the footsteps of my three brothers and took a part-time job while attending school. I worked during the daytime and studied in the evening at a technical school. My father died of cancer. At the time, I was not yet a legal adult. Traumatized and saddened by his death, I began to engage in quite a few unhealthy activities, such as gambling, drinking, fighting, reckless driving, gossiping, along with wasting my time thinking about horrible things.

I loved sports. I made use of mornings, my time after work, and before class to work out. According to my thinking at that time, sweating was a means of proving that I was still alive. I also participated in various tournaments and won many awards and prizes. I was exposed to many temptations and became absorbed in pursuing personal fame and gain. I gradually lost myself in it all. I spent all my time and energy attempting to climb to the top in my career. As a result, my family began to find it difficult to understand me. The trust between my friends and me was gone, and my health deteriorated as I pushed myself to the limit physically.

One day, an older friend of mine gave me a popular newspaper that contained some very positive and inspiring stories. Tears began to stream down my face as I was reading it on my way home in the subway. I read stories about being kind and learned many new things. One article I read was discussing Falun Gong practitioners being persecuted in China. Since I wished to know more, a few days later I began to read *Zhuan Falun*.

I joined a practice site in my neighborhood after I finished reading *Zhuan Falun* for the first time. Afterwards, something miraculous happened. I had never won any scholarships in my life, but after beginning to practice Falun Gong, I was awarded scholarships in three consecutive school terms! I realized that doing well in my studies was a result of the increased focus I had developed from practicing Falun Gong.

After a year of practicing Falun Gong, my brother's wife commented that I had changed immensely. She went on to say that I had become more down-to-earth and that I no longer focused on superficial things. My sister had also recognized that I was much more sensitive to other people and was always taking the initiative to help others. Moreover, my colleagues were amazed at how I had made such positive changes within such a short period of time. They said they admired my new commitment and devotion to work. In addition, my team members also observed that I was no longer the aggressive person I used to be. They also mentioned seeing other positive changes in me.

Lately, I have heard people comment on my youthful appearance. I could not help but recall an incident when I was in high school. One day, I went out with a friend. We saw his friend coming up to us, and she said to my friend, "Hi. So you are hanging out with your aunt?" I was totally shocked by what I heard and did not know whether to laugh or cry. I know that I owe the change in my appearance to Falun Gong. I know that it is a practice of mind and body, and that many practitioners experience significant improvement in their complexion, where it becomes fair and rosy. This occurs even with the elderly. If you are interested in Falun Gong too, you can read *Zhuan Falun* and you will find the answers you seek.

Overcoming Complacency To Become a Better Person

By Sharon Kilarski, Chicago, Illinois, U.S.A.

I have been a Falun Gong practitioner since late June, 1999. At that time I had already been doing the exercises for about three months but was also practicing Tibetan Buddhism. After listening to the nine-day lecture series, though, I struggled for a short time and decided to finally commit myself to just practicing Falun Dafa. I knew that I had been making no progress in cultivation up to that point. In looking back, although I'm still working towards becoming a better person and have a very long way to go, I have made certain progress in that direction.

I'm a second generation American, of mixed Polish and Russian-German ancestry. Although my family were non-practicing Catholics and Protestants, they instilled Christian concepts in me by clearly distinguishing what was right and wrong. Each of them had been raised by very religious mothers. Despite or because of my parents' humble backgrounds, growing up here during the Depression, they wanted their children to succeed in the material world, and so they considered doing well in school extremely important. As a child, I learned to compete for grades by the time I was in high school. At the same time, I had sense enough to be embarrassed by my own need to be the best. To compensate, I became not only good in school, but also good at analyzing my own faults (and others') and good at seeming like a wonderful person. I was very cheerful and helpful. I had a very altruistic point of view. By the time I was in graduate school, I had convinced many people of my goodness and certainly had convinced myself.

For this reason, practicing cultivation was hard for me. I was complacent with my life. I had always been treated well by others. Although my graduate studies added tremendous stress to my life, I was learning and intellectually stimulated. Although my husband and I worried about money, still he had a job and my stipend added a little to that, so that we always managed to pay the rent, eat and take care of our bills. I had many friends with whom I could indulge in gossip and good times. My life was good.

After finishing my comprehensive exams, my husband and I moved to Kansas City, where he found a better paying and more challenging job. I settled down to part-time work and to writing my dissertation. My contact with friends diminished, and the stimulating challenge of new projects and ideas did too. I still had a very optimistic attitude about life and progress because I considered the time in Kansas City as a stop-over on the way to something either more exciting or more familiar. At the same time, I began to reassess my progress as a cultivator.

Master Li gives us so much help that, after listening to the lectures for the first time, I felt like a different person. I could refrain from sarcasm when my husband got angry with me. I could monitor my own behavior more easily. And I literally could see the world in brighter colors.

As my cultivation began in earnest, I started on a tearful tour of realizing what I had become. For months, usually during the sitting meditation, I would have realizations that led me to cry. More accurately I would bawl. I would cry so hard that I'd get tired from it. I did not cry out of compassion for others. I cried out for all the bad things I had done. I cried when I realized that I'd been living a lie— that I had created an image of a wonderful and wise and loving person to show the world. I cried when I realized how kindly other people had treated me throughout my life. My parents tried to give me everything I wanted. My husband sacrificed years of his life in a job he hated in order to put me through school. I had often returned their kindness with smug indifference. I cried over and over again at my deeply embedded tendency to showing off. It seemed that everything I said was meant to show off in some way. I would be introduced to a new person, for example, and I would mention that I was working on my Ph.D. (As if they needed that piece of information!) While teaching my acting class (my studies are in theatre) and asking my students to sing a prepared piece of musical theatre, I managed to slip in a few bars of my own (as if I needed to impress junior high schoolers with my talents). All of these little events made me thoroughly unhappy with myself. This may not sound like a good way to be, but these feelings of remorse helped me considerably. I saw myself more truthfully and would vow never to show off again— until the next opportunity arose, and I would hear another inappropriate comment escape my lips. I battled and cried for three months in this way, and now I spend less time justifying my inconsiderate or self-interested behavior. I am beginning to recover some of the depth I had lost to glibness over the years. I have recovered some of the integrity instilled by my father and the compassion I had felt as a young child.

Some practitioners seem to have come from a past of despair or tortuous illness. I did not. I came from the other side and had to get past the easy world I had made for myself.

Today, I'm still struggling to become a better person. Nonetheless, what could be more precious than that struggle?

Take Hardships as Blessings, Look Inward for the Source of Our Difficulties

By Ye Ping, Boston, Massachusetts, U.S.A.

I have been in the United States for more than one year. Now, when I look back, I realize that I have experienced more hardships during this one year than in all the years since I started practicing Falun Dafa in 1995. I feel fortunate to have encountered these difficulties, because otherwise I would not have been able to improve my character.

I am a technician in my company. My responsibility is assembling and testing different kinds of micro-thermal equipment. In the early days, everything in the company was new to me, and I had to learn from my colleagues. I felt like I was being treated as an apprentice. I was ordered around to do all kinds of trivial work that no one else wanted to do. I had to endure people's impatience too. Whenever I ran into something new, I had to ask others. When I asked too much, they would get impatient, or if they happened to be in a bad mood, they would easily get impatient, too.

Different products have different procedures for assembly. If the procedures are not followed correctly, some problems may occur when the products are tested. This in turn might bring the company a big loss.

For a certain period of time, I made mistakes very often. Something always went wrong, even in an absurd manner. Sometimes, although I obviously followed the procedures very well and even got the green light from my colleagues, the results were still frustrating. Not surprisingly, I received a lot of harsh comments from the lab supervisor, which made me very sad. I thought to myself, "I'm trying to do my best. Is there anything wrong with that?" To make it worse, one of my colleagues always reported to the supervisor upon spotting even the tiniest mistake of mine. The supervisor would then get impatient immediately and shout, "You can't make mistakes all the time. Otherwise, I can't keep you here anymore." Then I would get angry too and think, "All human beings make mistakes. Do you think I made them intentionally?" At those times, my mind would be occupied by one idea, "Fire me, then. If worst comes to worst, I will go home. That's it. I'm fed up with this kind of life."

This situation continued for a long time, until one day I made an error just as the supervisor happened to pass by. He asked me what happened. I told him I made another mistake and expected him to explode with complaints. To my surprise, he went away without saying anything. All of a sudden, I felt awakened from a dream. So many days of reprimands and arguments all came out of one attachment: every time a mistake occurred, I had always remained silent and tried to cover it up. When someone came to inquire, I said that everything was fixed and fine. I always held the belief that so long as I ended up with a good result, everybody should be happy. They shouldn't bother asking what happened in the process. On the surface, my argument sounds reasonable. But to a Dafa practitioner, it is not. A practitioner should follow the principle of "Truthfulness", do things in an upright way, be willing to admit to any mistakes and be crystal clear regarding every matter. Isn't the attempt to cover up mistakes a big attachment? Surprisingly, after that event I seldom made mistakes. Consequently, the supervisor never complained again, and no one bothered to report my mistakes to him anymore.

Probably because no one in my family creates trouble for me, I was destined to encounter more trouble in my company so that I would have opportunities to cultivate. One colleague seemed very aggressive in every single matter. He had a habit of preempting the company's equipment, even if he had no immediate use for it. Therefore, when the time came that I needed to use a certain piece of equipment, I could not, and my work would be delayed. Besides, I'm a person of discipline and order and always keep my tools and equipment neatly assorted. He was just the opposite, leaving every piece of equipment messy, greasy and sometimes broken after he used it. At times when he could not find his own tools, he used mine and occasionally lost mine too. My work would then be greatly affected. Similar kinds of things happened to me almost every day. Several times I could not control my temper and burst into anger. Afterwards I regretted what I had done. On the issue of improving my character, when there were conflicts, I felt that I was moving up very slowly. Why couldn't I feel within myself a heart of compassion and kindness? If a trivial matter could hurt me, I was far from being firm and unmoved, as a Dafa practitioner should be.

After thinking about it, I understood why. In the first place, it was because I had adopted a biased attitude toward others. I looked at them as selfish, rough and unorganized in their work. I always had perceived things around me strictly from my own point of view. When others did not fit my perceptions, I felt uncomfortable with them. Why had I become so angry? It was because they disturbed my work and created trouble for me. Every bit of my thinking had been about myself only. Was that not selfish? If he had been making trouble for others, disturbing other people's work, I would not have become angry.

In every matter we must be considerate of others! After I started adopting such an attitude, I no longer felt annoyed by my co-workers. On the contrary, I started to feel compassion for them, because they, too, were suffering from the difficulties in their lives.

An American High School Student: "It Was My Heart and Mind That Needed To Change"

By Daniel Pomerleau, Maine, U.S.A.

I am 17 years old and have been a practitioner of Falun Dafa for about six months. At the time just prior to my cultivation, things were not going very well in my life, and I was both spiritually and mentally confused. Trying to fit into the ordinary way of life just didn't seem fulfilling and purposeful to me. I didn't know what to make of life and couldn't understand what I was to do with my life. Why was I here? What was the purpose of my existence? I had been brought up in a religion, but it never seemed to answer the questions I had, and I never seemed to fully connect with its teachings. I was very much lost, and I wished I had some practice to follow so I could find my way.

It was then, like clockwork, that my brother sent me a copy of *Zhuan Falun* in the mail. At first, I didn't know what to make of it. Being brought up in a small town in the Northeastern United States, I didn't know anything about cultivation practice, and some of the words in the strange blue book, let alone the title, which I couldn't even pronounce, were very foreign to me. Nevertheless, I was deeply intrigued by it and could hardly put it down. The more I read, the more questions Master Li answered, and the more my mind seemed to open up to the profound principles in the book. I could sense there was something very special, very powerful, and very profound about this book, and I felt I had found my way.

Shortly after, I experienced my first tribulation, although I didn't fully understand it at the time. I was going to a planetarium to see a laser light show with three of my friends. On the way there, I missed the exit to get on to the Interstate from the highway, and as a result, increased my travel time by about 20 minutes. In order to cope with this setback, I began to speed to try and make up for the lost time. When I got pulled over by a police officer, I got a speeding ticket, and on top of that, lost my license for two months. When we got to the planetarium, it was too late and we missed the show. On the way back home, while driving on the Interstate, I began to feel the car die out. It turned out that the car had run out of gas, even though the gas needle registered at over a quarter of a tank. I had to call my parents on a cell phone, and my dad had to come with some gas. Normally, because of my temper, I would have gotten into an argument with him, but because of what I had learned from *Zhuan Falun*, I was able to remain calm.

After that night, I continued to read *Zhuan Falun*. I finished reading the book in a couple of weeks, and after talking with my brother, began reading it again. Even without having a very good understanding of the Fa and without knowing anything about the five sets of exercises,

I knew in my heart that I wanted to be a practitioner of Falun Dafa and wanted to practice cultivation. I wanted to assimilate to the characteristic of the universe, *Zhen-Shan-Ren* (Truthfulness-Compassion-Forbearance), and return to my original, true self. In essence, the wish I had made had been granted, and I now had my way to follow.

When I first began my cultivation, I was very excited and very happy. My brother gave me the videotape of the five sets of exercises and I seemed to pick them up rather quickly. Although I couldn't sit in the full lotus position and couldn't hold the Falun Standing Stance Exercise for very long, I felt very content with myself during the practice. But because of my superficial understanding of the Fa, the things I began to give up and change about myself were all superficial as well. I understood attachments only as material things and understood cultivating character as having to do only with moral values. In addition, I wasn't using the Fa to measure myself with. With this poor understanding, I began to improve myself only on the surface. Of course, this needed to occur in order for me to become a good person, which is the first step towards becoming a practitioner, but as time passed, I didn't seem to be making much progress.

I read the book more, and it became evident to me that what I was doing was not true cultivation. Although I felt very good about myself and my practice, I was not truly giving up my deep-down attachments, the root causes for all of my problems. Because of this, my mind had become foggy and my thoughts unclear. In *Zhuan Falun*, Master Li says, "Whenever there is interference of one kind or another in qigong practice, you should look for reasons within

yourself and determine what you still have not let go."
(*Zhuan Falun*) I realized from this that I would have to give
up much more than just the superficial things if I wanted to
be a true practitioner and truly advance. It wasn't just my
actions and habits that needed to be changed and/or given
up, it was what was inside, my heart and my mind, that
needed to change. Without doing so, my character would
not be able to upgrade, and my cultivation would be in vain.

The time between then and now has been like a roller
coaster ride. I would make progress, then fall back down,
and make progress again, and fall again. But because of
those ups and downs, I have been able to learn a lot. In
fact, this is just the cultivation process. For instance, in the
beginning of my cultivation, every time I would understand
something new in *Zhuan Falun* or my exercise time would
increase, I would become excited and think, "Wow, I am
making good progress," or "Wow, I am doing really great."
I would then, without realizing it, become complacent, and
as a result, would fall back down. For quite a while this was
happening, then I realized that it was just because of my
attachment of complacency that I would fall back down after
making a little progress. Once I gave up this attachment, I
found that after making a little progress, I was able to keep
making more progress. Sometimes though, I feel myself
getting lazy, so I try to read the book every day and practice
when I can. Now, when my practice time increases, I think
to myself, "I should endure longer next time."

Recently, I went through a tough ordeal in my
cultivation. Over the course of several days, my mind
became more and more unclear, and the warm feeling
inside of me disappeared. I even began to doubt whether

or not I was able to cultivate. I didn't know why this was happening, but after reading a passage from *Falun Dafa, Essentials For Further Advances*, I found my answer. Master Li said, "I also want to tell you that your nature in the past was actually based on egotism and selfishness. From now on, whatever you do, you should consider others first, so as to attain the righteous Enlightenment of selflessness and altruism." ("Non-Omission in Buddha-Nature") Shortly after reading this, I realized that my thoughts over the past few weeks had become increasingly self-centered. I was only thinking about things relating to myself and not thinking of others, and my problems increased the more this happened. I would then begin to worry about it more and more, and in an effort to try and find out what the problem was, would become even more engrossed with myself, instead of paying attention to cultivating my character. In fact, it was the attachment of selfishness that was the problem. Once I realized this, a week of troubles disappeared in a second and it was as if I could feel Compassion bloom inside of me. After that, I didn't have a single selfish thought about myself, and could only think of others. It was a very good feeling.

I can now sit in the full lotus position, and my practice is much more solid. When I am practicing the sitting meditation, I feel a warm current flow over my entire body, and my skin usually gets warm and red. At school, I find myself very content. I just sit there quietly while the people around compete and fight for their own interests. I sit there with a peaceful mind, but also become very sad while watching them, because of what they are doing. I used to be just like them, and sometimes I want to jump up and tell them what they are doing is wrong, that there is so much more to everything than what they think. But because I am a practitioner, I know it is not my place to get involved in their troubles. I think the desire to get involved is actually tied in with the attachment of showing off. I know feeling compassion brings about such a sadness for people, but feeling compassion does not mean that I should get involved in their business. If I really want to help them, I should tell them about *Zhuan Falun*.

Recently, quiet a few people at my school have become interested in learning about Falun Dafa, and I have given away several books. I think it is really great that they are interested in it, and I smile from ear to ear when I think about the benefits they will get from it. To promote Falun Dafa is just such a good thing, and I think I need to take a step up in this aspect. In the time to come, I am going to try and get a reading group and practice site started, and try to get *Zhuan Falun* into bookstores in my area.

Sometimes I feel overwhelmed and feel that the cultivation ahead of me is just too difficult and complicated. I try and shut these thoughts out of my mind as soon as they crop up because I know that they are just my attachments and karma interfering with me. They don't want to be eliminated, so they resist against my cultivation. I must be firm in mind and determined to make it, and let my cultivated side prevail over my uncultivated side, as well as accept hardships to eliminate my karma. The more I do this, the less difficult my cultivation will be. When encountering a problem, I must remember that overcoming it is truly not that difficult, and it's just the false ideas and notions that I have previously formed that make it seem that way. If I can ignore these illusions and look at the problems with my cultivated side, then it will be no problem to overcome them, whatever they are, and I will be able to get that much closer to my original, true self. After all, Master Li said in *Zhuan Falun*, "After passing the shady willow trees there will be bright flowers and another village ahead." I also must take bigger steps in improving my character, and evaluate my every thought and action with the Fa.

"Teacher, I Want to Learn Falun Gong!" – A Disobedient Boy is Transformed by Falun Dafa

By a teacher in China

I am a primary school teacher who has practiced Falun Dafa for over four years. I work as the head teacher of a class. In my class there is a boy from a rural area who is notorious in the school for making trouble. He was enrolled late in my class in the third grade. He didn't understand anything, nor did he listen to the teachers in class. He couldn't write a word, nor could he solve a problem. It seemed that he didn't have a sense of how to study at all. On his final exams, he got 6 points in math and 11 in Chinese language (out of 100 each). Almost every day he would make some trouble, big or little, without a break. He caused the most difficulties for the teachers, and also was a big headache for me. I patiently counseled him several times to behave himself, and his father also tried both hard and soft tactics at home with him, but none of these methods produced any results.

During the Spring Festival of 2001, the staged "Self-immolation Incident" occurred in Tiananmen Square, under a scheme by Jiang Zemin and the Chinese Communist Party to frame Falun Gong. After the incident, I often thought of letting my students know the truth, but I could not speak out, even when the words were on the tip of my tongue. I worried that students in the country were unsophisticated and it was likely to get me into trouble if I spoke out. So I did not tell my students about the truth of the incident. Later on, I felt that as a cultivator, clarifying the truth to people is to help them to establish the right understanding of Dafa. Everyone has a right to know the truth, including every innocent child. They should not have to live in lies and deception.

So one day I explained the truth about Falun Gong to my students. At that time both my mind and tone were very calm, without any worries. After I finished talking, a student in the last row of the classroom raised his hand and shouted loudly, "Teacher, I want to learn Falun Gong!" I looked around and found surprisingly that it was that troublemaker. At the time I thought he was making mischief and said right away, "You sit down first, wait until afterwards." I did not take it seriously, since I thought it was impossible for him to truly want to learn. So I kind of forgot about the matter.

Soon it was April 10. The last class in the morning is my morality class. At the end of the text, there was an essay slandering Falun Dafa. I thought, I can't allow such an abominable article to poison the pure hearts of the children. So, I told some true stories to the class about Falun Gong teaching people to be good, and the great deeds of Dafa practitioners who hold firmly to the truth in the face of vicious persecution. After I completed the talk, this student again put up his little hand and shouted loudly, "Teacher, I want to learn Falun Gong, please teach me!" I saw his sincerity, and promised him I would.

Section One in the afternoon was my math class. No sooner did I finish explaining one example, than this student raised his hand, saying that he could do it. At that time I did not believe him at first because he never listened to teachers in his classes, nor was he able to solve any problems. I let him go to the blackboard and work on the problem. Surprisingly, he did it correctly. I asked him to do another one, and again he did it right. Other students were very surprised. I thought at the moment that although I did not talk much, the boy had already been affected by the righteous power of Dafa that lifts people upward. He wanted to be good himself! This is something that cannot be achieved by any external force. I was very excited. The mighty power of Dafa had already transformed him. On the same afternoon after school, he found me in my office, and asked me, "Teacher, is there any book for learning Falun Gong?" I said, "Yes, but you can't read it yet." He insisted on reading it, and wanted to know if he could read it through. He opened the book and saw "Lunyu" [the Preface to *Zhuan Falun*]. Unexpectedly he read through it and only failed to recognize a few characters.

He really began to study from then on. He listened to teachers attentively in class, and also started to do homework. Once the Chinese language teacher talked to me, surprised, "What happened to this boy? He began to study. He took a Chinese language test and surprisingly, he correctly answered many of the questions. He seems to be a different person! He is also obedient and no longer makes trouble every day."

Just like that, the little boy started on his cultivation path of returning to his original, true self. And from this I understood that by truly using reason, wisdom and a benevolent heart to tell people about Falun Dafa, and doing things without pursuit, one will naturally do well.

Giving Up the Attachment to Fame and Personal Gain

By Jian Tianlun, Boston, Massachusetts, U.S.A.

In May of 1997, while I was working in New York, I watched Master Li's entire set of the nine-day seminar tapes without sleep or rest. While I was watching, I rejoiced at being able to find this great teacher, and to learn the purpose of being a human and the principles of cultivation practice. Soon afterwards, I borrowed tapes of Master Li's various lectures and Dafa books.

Though I had read all the Dafa books and practiced the exercises daily, I did not understand cultivation practice in daily life. In the beginning, I seldom joined the local group studies or discussions, as I had read *Zhuan Falun* several times and thought that I understood it pretty well. Later, I did participate in group discussion, and I found that I also went through some tribulations faced by other practitioners. But I had not treated the tribulation as a practitioner should, and let it go. I did not try to understand, and was even confused. Why did other practitioners go through tribulations one after another, while I did not experience any? In fact, it was not that I did not face any tests, but rather that I did not act according to Dafa's requirements. When faced with a tribulation, I neither examined myself for the cause, nor did I accept it as an opportunity for progress. I would assess the difficulty in the manner of an ordinary person and look for a way out. Thus I missed again and again the opportunities for cultivation. Not until that day did I realize the importance of group study and group practice. In such a cultivation environment, practitioners are able to share cultivation experiences to encourage each other and to improve together. This is especially good for getting rid of our attachments and it is the fastest way for improving ourselves. Master Li said, "To tell you the truth, the entire cultivation process for a practitioner is one of constantly giving up human attachments."(*Zhuan Falun*) From then on, I began to regularly join group Dafa study and group practices.

In the past few years, competition between long distance telephone companies has become more and more intense. They employ various means to attract customers, such as rate reductions, monthly fee waivers, and even cash rewards. I also became one of their targets. Favorable terms given by one firm were bettered by another. At first, I was unwilling to switch telephone companies, because I did not want the trouble. It was also because I thought, "How can I get another's money with no good reason?" Then I was told that it only takes a few minutes to switch companies; we would not only enjoy lower rates, but also would get a cash reward. At that time, I was laid-off and did not have much to do, so I decided to give it a try. After such a try, I immediately felt the benefit. It was only two to three weeks after I switched companies, and another firm called me up and gave even more favorable terms. The company representative even said, "What are you worrying about?" I was saying to myself: It is not I who asked for it, and this is the way they do business. Don't worry about it, they are happy and I'm happy, too. So in just two months, I switched telephone companies three times and felt pleased with myself. Not long afterward, the telephone bill came. I looked at it. What was going on? How could only two to three long distance calls cost three hundred dollars? The firm had a rule that if customers switched to their firm and did not stay for a full three months, not only would they have to return the original cash award, but also they would be charged at the highest rate! With some calculation, I found all the money that I made by switching telephone companies had to be paid out now. I suddenly realized that as Master Li says: "No loss, no gain." I realized that this was a test to see if I coveted material gain. But I did not understand and failed the test. Instead I traded my virtue again and again in exchange for "favorite benefits," and did not treat myself as a practitioner.

This incident greatly exposed my attachment to material gain. I still remember when I first began to learn Dafa that I had said to myself the crux of Falun Dafa cultivation is to assimilate to the cosmic characteristic of Truthfulness, Compassion and Forbearance, and to get rid of human attachments to fame, material interest and sentimentality. At that time, I thought that I was not keen on fame or material interests. I thought my cultivation should focus on sentimentality. It seems now the so-called "not keen on fame or material interest" was simply from an average person's point of view. Having learned Dafa, I must live up to a higher standard.

I used to work in New York. Due to company restructuring, many of the staff members were laid off. I also lost my job, so I returned to Boston. I had just studied Dafa for two weeks. I wasn't very unhappy, and vigorously started to look for a new job. I thought that since I started late learning the Fa, such an arrangement would allow me time to catch up. From then on, every day, I would practice the exercises, read the Fa, and watch Master Li's lecture videotapes.

Half a year went by. Others had already found jobs, but I still had not settled down yet. It is not that there were no companies interested in me. In those few months, each month there were two to three job interviews. Some companies had even gone through all the procedures and were only waiting to choose a good date for me to begin the job. But for some unknown reasons, my starting date was postponed again and again. I simply could not start a new job. In the beginning, I found many objective reasons: the companies merged and so froze the payroll; managers left the company; the plan for new hiring changed, etc… I experienced every one of the above. Then there came the Asian Financial Crisis, and many financial firms began massive layoffs. For myself, who specialized in Asian economies, it was yet another blow. I considered myself to be a good person. I did not have strong attachments to fame or material interests. I did not seek high living standards. Wherever it is, whatever it does, as long as the job utilizes my specialty, and as long as the salary is commensurate with my experience and capabilities, I would be content. I did not realize, however, I was obstructed in the improvement of my character just because of such a way of thinking.

One night, I received a telephone call from an executive director of a large investment firm. He said that I was recommended to fill a position analyzing Asian economies and stocks. After we spoke briefly, I felt the job fit me very well, as it suited my strengths and specialty. He was also very satisfied and prepared to offer me an interview with his associates. But as we discussed further, a conflict emerged. On discussing the topics of Asian stocks and Asian economies, I totally forgot myself, as if I were an authority. I started talking bombastically, and even started to argue with him. Each sentence was filled with the mentality of showing off and the mentality of competing. My daughter described my conversation to me: "If it was written down, every word would be in bold and each sentence would have an exclamation mark!" After the telephone call had finished, my wife said, "With your way of talking, it would be surprising if anyone would hire you. You have had so many interviews, why were they all unsuccessful? You should look into yourself for answers." That's right. Master Li said that when there is a conflict you should look inward, instead of outward. How could I have spoiled such a great opportunity? Why? Recalling the entire course of the phone interview, I found that my words were filled with the attachment to fame. I exploited every opportunity to show that I was a professional and an expert. I was jealous that others were better than I was. Facing a conflict of opinions, I was arguing for my self-esteem to prove that "I'm right and you're wrong."

That night I thought a lot. Seeking fame, status, benefits and recognition from society are attachments to fame that are easily detected. Through studying the Fa, I have become less concerned about fame and material interests. But my attachment to fame had deep roots back to the days in elementary school when I began competing for rankings in school. After I started working, I was seldom satisfied with my own position and was always ready to switch to a better one. I always thought that I was better than others. I used every chance to flaunt my knowledge and abilities, and to have others see me as someone amazing and extraordinary. This kind of attachment to fame and material interests, compared to the kind mentioned above, is more subtle, and not as easily detected. That is why I used to always feel unfortunate and why I felt others didn't understand me. Only at this time did I recognize that according to the standard of Dafa, I not only did not relinquish the attachment to fame and material interests, but the attachment had been developing since my early years. Such attachments had deep roots, permeating every aspect of my life. Often, when I met a new friend or colleague, I would naturally ask which school he graduated from and the ranking of the department. Such attachments to fame also affected my child's education without my noticing it. There seemed to be a general understanding that she would not attend any colleges other than Harvard or MIT. This invisibly generated unnecessary pressure for her. And thus for some time she reported only the good news and not the bad, for fear that she might get criticized for not meeting her parents' expectation. Was I teaching her something good or bad?

Thinking about this, I suddenly realized that the entire process of finding a job was in fact the best opportunity to cultivate myself. In such a process, my attachments to fame and material interests were fully displayed to me. Through looking inward, my anger cooled. Not long afterwards, I finally got a position at a financial firm in Boston.

Master Li said: "As a human being, you are a good person only if you can follow this universe's characteristic of *Zhen-Shan-Ren*." (*Zhuan Falun*) Master Li also said: "As a practitioner, if you assimilate yourself to this characteristic you are one that has attained the Tao—it's just such a simple principle." (*Zhuan Falun*). After considering the three aspects, *Zhen, Shan, Ren* (Truthfulness, Compassion, Forbearance), I found that I was the worst at Forbearance. I had to work on Forbearance. But even then I didn't think carefully about why I could not forbear. I thought at the time that if someone hit me or cursed me I would probably be able to forbear because I had learned from reading the teachings that I had to forbear it. I also thought though that I may not be able to truly remain unmoved in my heart. I thought that I should improve step by step. Since my character did not improve, whenever a tribulation came, I would not be able to forbear. To save face, I would always grumble and talk back. It was only after the tribulation that I realized that I should have forborne. The reason why I couldn't stay unmoved in my heart was that I didn't improve my character and dig down to the fundamental reason why I could not forbear. After two years of cultivation I gradually realized that the reason I could not forbear was that I was still attached to fame and personal gain. When I encountered a tribulation I never looked inward but I always looked externally for reasons, trying to give myself some evidence that I was right. That was why I had to reason with others until they agreed with me. If I couldn't reach my goal then it was impossible for me to continue to forbear. Outwardly it is not being able to forbear, yet from a deeper level of understanding it is also not possessing enough compassion.

Saving face exposes the attachment to fame. When one competes and fights to save face, or to protect his own material interests, one will not consider saving face for other people, nor will he think of others first all the time and he won't be compassionate to others. So that's why there is compassion in forbearance, and why, when I didn't possess enough compassion, I would not be able to be broad-minded either, nor be able to always forgive others' mistakes, nor be able to let go of my material interests. As a practitioner I should act as Dafa directs and think more of others. Only in this way will I be able to look inward when encountering tribulations. In the process I shall upgrade my character, remove all my attachments, assimilate to the cosmic characteristic, Truthfulness-Compassion-Forbearance, and quickly return to my true self.

Growing with the Fa

By Maria McMullan, Ireland

Women of all ages have a reputation for often looking in the mirror to see how they look, if their hair is right or if their clothes are right. Men do this too, but seldom admit to it. How we think and feel about others does not show in the mirror. Neither does it show if we are good or bad. It only reflects what we look like on the surface and how we appear to others.

Since becoming a Falun Gong practitioner, I have learned to look inward. The Fa is a great mirror for showing how I look on the inside. I can't hide any attachments, faults, anger, jealousy, unkindness or lack of compassion from the Fa. If I haven't taken the trouble to be nice to someone, just because I feel a bit tired, the Fa lets me know. If at any time I don't think or act as a cultivator, the Fa lets me know. The Fa has become the guiding force for who I am and I feel that I am surrounded by it. If I have a thought to take a day off work because I feel tired, I remember Master Li's words saying that we "must do everything well."

However, this mirror works both ways. It also shows me

how I have improved my character, my way of thinking, my attitude towards others and my way of looking at life. The Fa is a divine light, which clearly shows me how to apply Dafa principles in my heart, thoughts and deeds. However, it can only work if I open myself to it and not get lost in the midst of mundane issues.

Before I knew about Falun Dafa my life was much different. I worked hard and was very ambitious to be successful. I measured success by how intelligent a person was, how good a job they had, how hard they worked or how well educated they were. I admired smart people and wished that I could be smarter. I felt that this was what people needed to be in order to be good parents and in order to set an example for their children. I was quite judgmental about those who didn't work or didn't educate their children properly. I had come from a poor background and didn't get to go to college. So, over the years I educated myself by attending courses, studying for diplomas and such, until I came to realize that this just made me a more informed person, but not necessarily a better person.

There was always something missing, but I didn't know what it was. I studied several religions and even took study lessons with these religious groups. I needed something to believe in, but I wasn't aware of it all the time.

While shopping in Drogheda with my husband a little over two years ago, we saw a group of young Chinese people collecting signatures for Falun Dafa. We read the posters about the persecution and signed the petition. We also brought home some leaflets. I was very impressed with the peacefulness of these young people, some of whom were sitting in meditation. It was very beautiful.

My husband searched the Internet for more information about Falun Dafa. I thought it was just another type of exercise group, so I didn't pay much attention. My husband downloaded the exercises and started to practice. I still didn't pay much attention, as he has always been interested in physical exercise. When the time spent exercising increased from one to two hours each night, I began to feel a bit resentful and ended up having a row with him. Then he asked me to try exercising with him, saying it would be good for my health. I had chronic asthma and was on medication most of the time. I also had been in the hospital three times over a period of eighteen months. My lung had collapsed; I could hardly breathe and was eventually sent home with strict orders to use a nebuliser machine and to take steroids.

I began to practice the five exercises and each time after the second exercise, "Holding the Wheel," I was able to breathe easily for the first time in years. All my muscles relaxed and I felt able to take deep breaths without coughing all the time. When I was given Master Li's book, *Zhuan Falun*, it took me six weeks to read the first chapter, because I didn't read it diligently. When I got to the second chapter I felt as though I couldn't read it enough. I knew that this was what had been missing in my life. The exercises now had meaning and I had no doubts about Master Li's teachings. I did have a problem understanding some of the Fa, but I knew from speaking to other practitioners that if I continued to read and study I would eventually understand. From *Zhuan Falun*, I understood that if I cultivated diligently and began to elevate my character, I could become a Falun Dafa practitioner. Each chapter opened new insights for me and I was determined to be a good practitioner and cultivator.

I started to go with some practitioners to where a class was being held. It was here that I gained enough confidence to practice the exercises in front of others. I still was worried about looking foolish if I did the exercise incorrectly. I was impressed by the kindness of the practitioners in the way they corrected my posture or my movements. I learned how to do the five exercises properly. They are very graceful, but very powerful and effective. One day I was doing some housework, and I went into my bedroom. This was the day that I realized that I no longer needed all the medication I was taking. I got a large box and threw out all of my medication, including the nebulizer machine. I had been practicing for about three months at this time, and since then have never needed any medicine, a doctor or a hospital. My health has greatly improved.

I then started to go to the group practice at Dublin City University every Sunday. There was a beautiful feeling within the group. Each time I felt energized and determined to cultivate well.

I have been a practitioner for just two years now. In that time my life has changed dramatically. My fundamental thinking has changed. I now teach the classes in Trinity College in Dublin every Tuesday and Thursday night, with the help of other practitioners. I have traveled to other parts of Ireland to introduce Dafa to others, and handed out leaflets so as to give people the opportunity to know about Falun Dafa.

For the first time in my life there is a sense of belonging and knowing my way home. The road is long, but only as difficult as I make it. Master Li has shown me the way and now it is up to me.

Stories of Young Beibei from China

By a practitioner in China

In May 1997, Beibei started to practice Falun Dafa along with his mother. At the time he was 9 years old. Dafa is now deeply rooted in his heart. The following are some of the stories from his practice.

One day in September 1997, Beibei accidentally bumped into a classmate who was holding a cup of steaming hot water. The water was spilled and scalded the classmate's hand. Angrily the classmate poured the remaining water onto Beibei's chest, causing bad burns that blistered immediately. Despite the injustice, Beibei kept silent and didn't blame the boy. Other classmates were scared by the injury and called the teacher. The teacher informed the other student's parents, and together they went to Beibei's home.

Beibei's mother asked about what happened, but she mainly consoled the teacher and the classmate's parents without blaming them. Beibei said to his mother, "I feel bad about bringing so much trouble to the teacher..." Hearing this, the other student's parents and the teacher were too moved to say anything. "We were prepared to face anger," said the other student's parents, "but now we feel so ashamed."

That night, when Beibei lay down to sleep after finishing his homework, his mother asked him, "Do the burns hurt?" "No," answered Beibei. To a cultivator, one thought is often the difference between a good or bad outcome. The next morning, the blisters had disappeared, and the skin looked normal. After that, the trouble-making student was no longer as badly behaved as before.

In 1999, Beibei was attending his second semester of middle school. He ranked among the top five on the middle school entrance exam.

One month after the beginning of the new semester, Beibei's mother went to appeal on behalf of Falun Gong in Beijing. Afterwards, Beibei and his father also appealed. They were arrested, and the three family members were sent back home on the same day. Beibei's father was sent to a labor camp, while he and his mother were taken to the local 610 Office. Seeing the sad look on his mother's face, Beibei encouraged her by saying, "Mom, don't worry. I'll go to school all the same, but you must not write any statements promising to give up Falun Dafa." This shocked everyone in the room. His mother was sent to a detention center. It is hard to imagine that an 11-year-old child would be forced to live alone.

Although he had never been to his grandmother's house before, Beibei took the bus there alone and brought his grandmother back to his home. Arriving back in school, the principal and the teachers talked with him one by one, urging him to give up practicing Falun Dafa. Beibei said, "I should not lie." Under pressure, his teacher said sternly, "You'll be expelled if you don't write the promise." Beibei, however, remained firm in his faith. At home, Beibei's grandmother and many other relatives anxiously tried to persuade him to write a fake promise to stop practicing, but Beibei firmly insisted that following "Truthfulness, Compassion and Forbearance" and striving to be a good person were not wrong. He refused to speak any lies against his conscience.

Over the last three years, the persecution of Falun Dafa practitioners by the Chinese Communist regime has continued to escalate. Beibei has been forced to live without the care of his parents and has borne tremendous hardship. On December 5, 2001, Beibei's mother was arrested again for distributing materials that expose the truth about the persecution of Falun Gong. His father was still in a labor camp. The police officers brought his mother to their home, ransacked it, and stole a computer and other materials. His mother was handcuffed as Beibei watched. They sent Beibei's mother to a detention center, leaving Beibei without his parents once again.

The neighbors all knew that Beibei's mother was a good person, so they helped to look after Beibei while she was being held in the detention center. Once, Beibei went to visit his mother, and he comforted her by saying, "I am fine, neither hungry nor cold." His mother relaxed a lot in her heart and became more determined in the jail. She fearlessly and continually clarified the truth to the criminals and wardens, thus benefiting those people's future. After conducting a hunger strike, his mother was finally released unconditionally on April 19, 2002. But the 610 Office still refused to leave her alone. Ten days after her release, she was forced to leave home to avoid arrest. Beibei had to part with his mother yet again, but he was proud of her when he told her story to his classmates. His father kept clarifying the truth to the guards at the labor camp and was very determined to remain steadfast in his belief. He was released at the end of his sentence.

Discovering Hope In the Sea of Misery --
A Young Man Finds Falun Dafa in Prison

By a practitioner in China

In October 1999, I received a prison sentence and suddenly became a convict. Originally, even the prosecutor said that I should be found innocent. My lawyer also said that I was innocent and that if I were to be found guilty, he would not charge me a penny. Nevertheless, I was found guilty and the next thing I knew, I was in prison. I could find no one to share my pain or listen to my complaints. I felt heartbroken.

In December 1999, several groups of Falun Gong practitioners were sent to the same prison simply for upholding their faith. At that time I did not understand the practitioners' efforts in their cultivation practice. Together with other inmates, I laughed at them, thinking that they could find nothing better to do but bring trouble upon themselves. I even said that Falun Gong practitioners had mental problems. I also speculated that they were politically motivated. After I was moved to different cells, these questions were gradually resolved. During my time in the prison, I was moved seven times. Each move provided an opportunity to meet more practitioners.

Prison is pure hell. Everything, from daily life to people's thinking, is very different from the outside world. Inmates fight for food, spread gossip and mock each other. In prison, people do whatever they can to make themselves feel good at others' expense. The only exceptions were the Falun Gong practitioners. They never fought back when attacked, either physically or verbally. They cared for other people. They placed value on virtue and good deeds. They also clarified the truth about Falun Gong, patiently advising the criminal inmates to become good people.

In the seven months I spent in prison, all the practitioners I knew were the same way. Regardless of their education level, they all demonstrated a high moral standard. They had a great capacity to tolerate differences in people, and they all were able to endure tremendous hardships. Their sincere manner and compassion were most memorable. After spending time with Falun Gong practitioners, I was amazed that I could meet such good people in such a dark place. Under their great Teacher's guidance, they were practicing a wonderful cultivation. I secretly admired them. Falun Gong practitioners are the most fortunate people in the world.

This experience taught me an important lesson. I established an upright understanding of the world and found the true meaning of life. I saw a light in the darkness and found truth in that boundless sea of misery. I am grateful to those who put me in prison, even though their motives were personal revenge. How else could I have ever met so many Falun Gong practitioners? Without this experience, I would have taken more wrong turns in life and committed more bad deeds. This prison term for me was a blessing in disguise. Why do I say this? Because I have learned Falun Gong! I will tell my family and friends about the persecution. I will invite them to practice Falun Gong. I will tell everyone to remember Truthfulness-Compassion-

Forbearance. I will tell them that Falun Dafa is great.

Now people around me tell me that I am a different person. They say that I have more respect for people. That is because when I was in prison, I read *Zhuan Falun*, the main book of Falun Gong. After I heard Falun Gong practitioners clarifying the truth about the persecution, I vowed to start practicing Falun Gong after getting out. Later on, I became a Falun Gong practitioner myself.

Now I am telling everyone my own experience: Please try to find out more about Falun Gong practitioners. Please come to learn the truth about Falun Gong!

Becoming More Mature in My Practice of Falun Dafa

By Nadine Leichter, New York City, New York, U.S.A.

It has been almost two years since I began practicing Falun Dafa, and in that time I have encountered unending opportunities for growth and wisdom. As a practitioner, upholding the universal principle of Truthfulness-Compassion-Forbearance is a challenging and sacred commitment. More and more, the power this principle has to transform is revealing itself to me. In April 1999, when I started on the path of cultivation, I mainly focused upon acting according to the highest standard of these three words, maximally giving up attachments, and practicing and studying well. While there certainly was nothing incorrect with that approach, I can see now that the main emphasis of those activities centered on the words "my cultivation" and what that meant to me, how it benefited me, improved me, and helped me. In fact, just admitting this, I feel ashamed and can see my attachment to self-centered thinking.

In my daily life, I have a difficult job, full of difficult people. Sometimes they go to great lengths to be disruptive just to prove the smallest point. Many of them seem to be locked in a struggle for what they can get at the expense of everyone else. When I began working at my job, I had just begun practicing Falun Dafa and set forth to be very diligent about maintaining my principles and being a good person. Working in this harsh and competitive environment was very painful and almost unbearable. I felt terrible seeing the worst in people. My level of understanding at the time caused me to decide that I should forbear all difficult matters and work diligently without complaint. This is what I thought a good practitioner should do, so I steadfastly set upon this task and then immediately my tests began.

At work, as I became more preoccupied with finding new ways to forbear my environment, more unreasonable tests came my way. I endured so many ridiculous things it makes me laugh now, such as the time I was completely soaked in a rainstorm on my way to work. I arrived late with an inch of water in each shoe. My boss reprimanded me for arriving late and then, without any consideration for my soaking wet condition, insisted that we begin work (although he did let me pour the water out of my shoes). I was forced to work with him all day in a room where he kept the air-conditioning on full blast because he felt too warm. Meanwhile I was shivering with cold and I didn't dry off until it was time to leave. My heart was really heavy at his selfish actions, but I continued to forbear.

Another time, several individuals created a big problem after not taking responsibility for an important issue. This resulted in a huge and potentially expensive problem. Instead of reporting their mistake to the president, I quietly worked to fix the problem. It took three months of working late just to resolve it. In the end, I didn't receive any thanks;

instead, the people I had helped told the president that I had made the mistake! I felt very angry but still didn't say anything and kept on forbearing.

It just kept continuing in this way. When people told distasteful jokes in the office I would leave the group, eat lunch by myself, or not talk to them unless I had a good reason. At the time I felt I was acting as a good practitioner but actually I was avoiding my cultivation environment. The more I would forbear, the more problems I would have. I began to avoid people and conflicts more and more and then tried to forbear more and more. Things just became worse. People constantly made me uncomfortable and acted tense around me. I was forced to work unreasonable hours. Then I began getting blamed for others' mistakes even as I was doing good deeds and fixing all their problems. I couldn't enlighten to what was going on. All types of miscommunications occurred with other practitioners. Through all of this I couldn't look within myself very well. I would make an attempt to find my faults but I would always see myself as a good practitioner. Unknowingly, I felt I was better than all those people. I was always worrying about their effect on my practice and tried to avoid letting them disturb or influence me in any way. I complained so much about how difficult things were for me and how unfair it was that I was always blamed. Now I can see just how much it had to do with my selfishness and the thought that I was better than those around me.

After enlightening to that realization I felt very humble and ashamed of myself. I made the decision that I would only acknowledge the good in everyone I worked with and not judge or criticize them. I sincerely appreciated their strengths and what I could learn from them. As soon as I held that thought, my boss hired someone to help me at work and my long hours were reduced. From taking this new attitude I noticed a kinder nature appearing in myself and I laughed more often. Suddenly my boss started joking more and smiling more. One day he even made a joke that when something went wrong everyone should just blame me for it. I really laughed at that because I could hear our Teacher using those words to point out an important issue—that a practitioner should always look inside for the cause of any conflict. Because of that I felt a lot kinder to those in my office and decided to appreciate my co-workers for helping me improve.

The environment in my job drastically changed for the better after I told my co-workers that I was a Dafa practitioner and explained about the persecution in China. This was a very general discussion and I worried it was not enough. In the past, no one knew very much about me and I kept all my personal business strictly to myself. I held the idea that my co-workers were too impossible to be able to understand or respect Dafa. But again I was wrong

In the past, if I had some Dafa activity or reading group to attend and my job required me to stay late at the last minute, I felt very resentful. After telling people I was a practitioner, the amount of respect they had toward me greatly increased and everything became more harmonious. I think it was because I finally showed them my heart instead of hiding and protecting it. For the most part they stopped swearing in the office in front of me, but even when they did I was still kind to them and didn't treat them harshly. When my boss was unreasonable or petty I told him how much I learned from him and appreciated the challenges he had to face. All of these things I did from a heart of sincerity. Suddenly, not only did the atmosphere in the office improve but people also began to share interesting things about themselves or show me their best sides.

This week I learned that a co-worker with a reputation for being confrontational who has always tried to undermine me took the time to do something for me that saved me much time and effort. What was amazing is that he did it without trying to take any credit or brag about doing it. That was so unbelievable that I cried when I thought about his change of heart that allowed him to put down his usual way of acting and do something unconditionally out of kindness. Previously I had wanted to leave my job so I could find an easier one and have more time for cultivation. Now I realize that I already have the best cultivation environment of all.

Over the past few months I have gained a new level of understanding of what cultivation is about. I have completely stopped worrying about the time and space for my personal cultivation and just want to take advantage of cultivation opportunities, meeting all conflicts with an unmoved heart. In fact this attitude has improved my cultivation and removed obstacles faster while my environment has become better and better.

As I learned this past year, the next step after personal cultivation is to achieve a more mature view. The concepts that have helped me to improve the most have included putting others' interests first, looking for the opportunity to improve in every activity, and choosing to act based on what is right from the Fa-principles, not from what I think is right or prefer to do. In all matters I try to act with a heart of true compassion, and in doing so I assume that I personally can make a difference instead of waiting for others to take care of the job.

In my understanding, all the worries about not having time, who is irritating you, and whether or not you can or can't do something are irrelevant. In becoming a more mature practitioner, I have opened my compassion, raised my level of wisdom, and learned that forbearance means maintaining the highest standard under all circumstances, not just enduring something painful. I feel that my understanding has become deeper. I just hope that I can do even better.

The Principles of Falun Dafa Helped Me Solve a Problem at Work

By Wen Jing in the U.S.A.

I work as a technician in charge of productivity in a small company. In order to squeeze out more time, I increased my efficiency and tried to finish my work while still guaranteeing quality, so that I could spend all my remaining time participating in activities to help end the persecution of Falun Gong in China. In recent years, there have been many such activities, and there are often urgent events that require me to take temporary leave from work. The whole year had been like this without any problems until recently. It was Orientation Day, in which different community associations promote their own culture. Of course, Falun Dafa practitioners also wanted to participate in the event. There was nobody at work who could replace me, but fortunately, there were enough practitioners to attend the event. Therefore, I was considerate of the company and decided not to attend this activity. Yet there was very little to do at work that day, and I finished before half the day was over. During lunch hour, I sat at my desk and a thought came into my mind: "Why not leave now?" I then emailed my deputy manager to request half a day of leave, and hastily left before she returned from lunch.

When I returned to work the following day, the deputy manager said to me, "According to your contract, you should stay in the office for 8 hours a day. According to company rules, you need to give two weeks notice before taking leave. Your behavior has violated your contract and the company is very unhappy about it! The company has no interest in keeping such an employee." Our deputy manager is a strong woman at work. A few months after she joined our company, our department manager resigned due to conflicts with her. She complained that the department manager was not productive enough. Thereafter, I became the only worker in the department.

Prior to practicing Falun Dafa, I was a hotheaded person. Unfortunately, I did not change much after I practiced. I had always thought that the company should reward me for doing the work of two people on my own. I had already been considerate of the company in not taking the whole day off. Furthermore, I had already finished my duties for the day. Why wasn't I allowed to take half a day off? Therefore, I told the deputy manager, "You should look at the company records. I have finished in one day what other employees take two days to do. My efficiency should win me some flexibility in work hours. What happened yesterday was an exceptional case, so why should you take it so seriously?" She said, "After you finish your own work, you could help others with their work. While you are at work, all your time must be devoted to work-related duties; otherwise you have breached your contract." Since she put such strong emphasis on the matter of working hours, while I was talking about efficiency, it was impossible for us to come to an agreement. Because of this, I suggested consulting the manager.

The next morning, the manager said to me that as a rapidly growing company, it was necessary to have strict requirements for management purposes. Every employee needed to abide by certain rules. Of course, on the other hand, the company is very respectful of employees' interests and habits. Take Falun Gong, for example: He said, "The company is very supportive of Falun Gong, yet it is not right for you to violate the company rules so often." I asked if the company could list my violations of punctuality. "You can't," I said. "I have been in the company for over a year now, and all you can remember are just three or four exceptional cases. Why do other people have flexible work hours, whereas even when I have finished my duties, I am still not allowed to enjoy any flexibility in my hours?"

It felt as though we had reached an impasse, and I could feel a strong field between us that would not allow us to come together.

I calmed down and took a few deep breaths, which allowed my mind to become more aware. I told myself, I am a practitioner, and Master Li has taught us to be good employees at work. What is wrong with me today? If other people are trying to find fault in me, there must be something I have missed as a practitioner. We should look inside under all circumstances; this is the fundamental difference between a practitioner and an everyday person. All the employees in our company are actually supportive of Dafa, and no one complains if I browse the Clearwisdom website every day. Before, our deputy manager had never accused me. What was the reason today?

Master Li's words suddenly came into my mind. We should consider others more under all circumstances. As Chinese practitioners living in the West, we should respect the habits of Westerners and the way they like to deal with things. For example, Chinese people would think it is not a big deal whether or not we hold the door for others; everyone can open their own door when they need to. Yet Westerners take this as a sign of good manners and respect for others. I suddenly understood where the problem was: the deputy manager was angry because I did not inform her early enough before I left work. I did not respect her in this sense. I acted first and reported afterwards, which hurt her pride.

I apologized to her sincerely, and explained the different customs and habits between the East and West. I also promised to ask for her permission before doing something like that in the future. I also explained to her the purpose of our activities and that time is very urgent at this point. I stressed again that I had increased my efficiency but I did not expect any monetary returns; all I would like is to win some spare time to do Dafa work. Soon, I could feel an obvious change in the atmosphere. The deputy manager's attitude had softened a lot. At last the manager said to me with a smile, "You won this time. Go and have your contract rewritten, to allow you some flexibility in your hours. I believe you will do your work well."

Not only did I not expect the conflict to be resolved so quickly, but I had also won the right to do Dafa work openly. Thinking back on this little story, I came to a clearer understanding of why it is important for us to act according to a cultivator's standard.

On the other hand, it is certainly necessary for those practitioners who do not have a flexible work schedule to treat their employer correctly and spend their work hours on their work. We should be considerate of others and earn people's respect everywhere we go.

A Small Video Clip Changes a Life

By a Chinese practitioner in the U.S.A.

I have been practicing Falun Dafa for a year and a half now.

Although I know the importance of clarifying the truth to Chinese people who have been deceived by the Chinese Communist Party, especially those who are from Mainland China, I often get unfriendly reactions and words from them that make me reluctant to try harder, and I often think, "I've tried my best."

Then my mother came to visit me from China a few months ago, and I had no choice but to face this big challenge. She was upset when she learned that I practice Falun Dafa and didn't want to hear any of the truth from me. Each time we ended our discussions, it was in a fight. I was worried for her, but my character was not yet improved enough to talk to her in a peaceful and intelligent manner. Whenever she quoted something from the evil propaganda, I got emotional. I gave up on her quickly and didn't want to try anymore.

But then, one day, I had to make some video copies for a fellow practitioner. It took me a while to set up the equipment. When I was finished, I started recording. Just then my mother happened to come into the family room to see what I was doing. She was immediately attracted to the beautiful three-minute Dafa exercise demo and sat down to watch it. I recorded it three times, and she watched it each of the three times without even moving. For the rest of the night and the next day, she sat on the couch and watched every Dafa film I recorded. One after another, changes began to take place in her.

After she watched the tape about the staged "self-immolation" in Tiananmen Square, she could not stop condemning the Chinese Communist regime for deceiving millions of its innocent citizens. While watching the tape about Zhang Cuiying, an artist who was imprisoned and tortured in China, her eyes watered. When she saw white, black, and Indian faces among the people doing the exercises, she was astonished and her chin dropped. After she watched the videos of Falun Dafa in Taiwan, she asked me what a nine-day seminar was and if she could attend one, too. Soon afterwards, we watched the nine-day seminar together.

Now my mother has begun practicing Dafa. She listens to Master Li's Fa lectures on CD every day while cooking, cleaning, and knitting. She reads Master Li's books every night. She tries to improve her character like a practitioner. Seeing the changes in her, I felt the immense power of Dafa. And to think that her amazing changes all started with a small Falun Dafa video clip that had no words in it.

Looking back at my previous mindset, I felt so ashamed. I was so uncompassionate. Now I can see that people still have a good conscience, but their good conscience is deeply buried under the lies and garbage that have been forced upon them by the Chinese Communist Party. It's all up to us to make the effort to clear it away and reveal the goodness in them.

There are millions of people in China just like my mother. Recently my mother said to me, "The poor people in China know nothing but lies." Her words gave me great confidence and courage to try harder in clarifying the truth to Chinese people. I no longer feel reluctant to speak about the truth of Falun Dafa. When I speak, my mother speaks the truth with me by telling her own story. Looking at the change in my mother, I can't stop thinking, "Dafa's power is so boundless!"

Viewing the World Differently Through Dafa

By a Western practitioner in the U.S.A.

My cultivation journey began in March of 2000. I had no idea at the time what I was undertaking. I couldn't believe how many insights and truths I read in *Zhuan Falun* when I first started practicing Falun Gong. I have to admit I did not believe everything I read at first. Some of it seemed so far out and was hard to comprehend. But other things I read I knew were truth. I also had a little problem with some of the concepts, but I just kept keeping on. Each time I read the book, I understood a little more. I just knew deep down I had to trust and that gradually my understandings would keep upgrading, which they did. For a time, I didn't know each day if I were going to keep practicing or not.

It was like being led down an unfamiliar path with the only connection being my heart. Nothing was familiar and it was faith that led me. I knew I had to keep open minded. It would have been so easy to quit and go back to my old ways of never really cultivating one way, but floundering and always searching.

All of my close friends were excited about Falun Dafa when it was first taught to us, including my husband. We all thought the energy felt great when we did the exercises together, and we were all pretty faithful doing them for about 6 weeks. Then little by little, as time went by they all fell by the wayside. I think the reason most people didn't continue is because they realized how many old patterns and habits they had to change to become true practitioners, and also the discipline it took. I know it wasn't easy for me, especially giving up all kinds of attachments.

When my husband saw how dedicated I had become, he got very hostile and angry, and even said bad things about Dafa. I really had to look within to see what caused this. After many tribulations with my husband, I have become so much stronger in who I am as a Dafa practitioner. We talked about it together, and it helped me to understand my husband's side more, and I have been more compassionate and tolerant towards him and his needs. He in turn had let go of his anger towards Dafa. He has been able to understand better my deep commitment and is much more tolerant of my beliefs. It would have been easy to blame him, but it is not one sided—we both had things we needed to work on, and we still do. Even though my husband doesn't practice Dafa, I feel my practice also helps him in many ways. I know he realizes now how good Dafa is because of my actions. If we Dafa practitioners walk our paths well, others will see our compassion and kindness, and through these actions we will show the goodness of Dafa.

One thing I have noticed is that I don't have ups and downs so much anymore. I'm more on an even keel. I don't try to fight life anymore but just let things happen. I also don't have expectations like I used to. I just do what my heart draws me to do without expecting any results. It makes life so much smoother.

Another aspect of the greatness of Dafa is my clarity of mind. From reading, studying and sharing, I know what is right and wrong and I know what has to be done to upgrade my character and become a better person. I don't have to guess. I also have a lot more compassion for other people because of the understanding I have gained from studying Falun Dafa.

I have gained so much from reading about the experiences of other practitioners, especially the Chinese practitioners, on the Clearwisdom.net website. I am very grateful to them and have great respect for their courage. They made me realize how small my hardships are compared to theirs.

Because of Master Li's teachings, my whole view of the world has changed. I have much to learn, and I will keep working on improving my understanding.

Rising from the Depths

By a Chinese-American practitioner in California, U.S.A.

I am a 26-year-old man, and I want to talk about my experiences after I began practicing Falun Dafa. I was a typical young Chinese American from California. My whole family immigrated to the United States in 1989 from the southern part of China. After I arrived here, I gradually changed into someone that wasn't recognizable as me at all. For example, I took up smoking, drinking, and going to nightclubs. I even got involved with a group of gangsters in Chinatown. Fortunately I did not commit any crimes involving fighting or shooting, although I used some fake credit cards to buy expensive things and stole change from parking meters.

In 1997 or 1998 when I was doing nothing, I went to the library one day and spotted a golden book called *Zhuan Falun*. I was interested because I had heard about it before, even though I didn't remember from where, so I checked the book out along with the exercise video. At first I thought it would be a really complicated book, but it was not. Instead, it used the most common language, yet contained the most profound explanations of the universe. I was really amazed and full of wonder at the book. I started reading it and finished it within days. At the time, I did not completely believe everything it contained, but I knew it was really good, so I started practicing some and following the requirements with respect to elevating my character. But I was a typical, lazy person, so I couldn't keep practicing every day. Eventually I stopped altogether.

In 1999 I watched the news on Chinese TV when China started persecuting Falun Dafa. I didn't believe the news from China at all, but due to the very limited understanding I had gained, for a very short time I had some doubts about Dafa. But after I read the book again, I couldn't find anything bad in it at all—it was a pure book from Heaven. However, human beings have a lot of reasons and attachments to give themselves all kinds of excuses not to follow the Fa. I was like this.

In the next two or three years, I took up another really bad habit: smoking marijuana. I don't know why, but I didn't want to face reality anymore, and marijuana gave me that escape. I felt so happy and detached when I smoked, and in my deluded state of mind, sometimes even wondered if this was what achieving Enlightenment was like. In the beginning I smoked once a month, then it was once a week, then once every couple of days, until finally I found myself smoking marijuana every day! Eventually I spent all my money. I knew it had to stop, but instead I stole money from my parents to buy more marijuana, while telling myself that I would stop after just one more time. But who was I kidding? I ended up smoking marijuana non-stop every day for almost two years.

One day I had spent all my money, including the money I had stolen from my parents. I knew that if I didn't stop right away, it was all over for me, so I decided to put an end to this once and for all. I went online to the Clearwisdom.net website. After reading some of the new articles from Master Li and some from the students, I realized how selfish and how bad I was. I swore to myself I would start over again.

Since then, I read all the articles on the Clearwisdom website every day, do two hours of practice at night, and go to bed reading Zhuan Falun before I fall asleep. It was not easy the first day I started again, especially when I was doing the second exercise. Maybe I had been too lazy in the past, but sweat dripped from my forehead to my chin, as if my hands were lifting thousands of pounds. In my mind I kept telling myself to stop and leap onto the comfy bed, but visions appeared of the students in Mainland China practicing every day, even in jails, with the prisoners and the police beating them up— but did they quit? No! The words from the books of Master Li also appeared, telling me that practice is hard, and if I could not even endure these little hardships, how could I practice cultivation? Who was I kidding? Thus, I didn't stop my practice. I followed the Falun Dafa music and finished the whole two hours. It's been about a month since the day I decided to start practicing cultivation. During this time, the urge to smoke cigarettes and marijuana cropped up a couple of times, but I kept reading the articles from Clearwisdom and *Zhuan Falun*.

Another thing happened two days after I decided to start practicing cultivation again. My best friend called me to go out and smoke marijuana like we usually did. I went with him, but after we smoked, I was very regretful that I had done it again. I realized that this was a test and that

I had failed. I decided to tell my friend that I had started practicing cultivation. I told him that I had quit smoking cigarettes and that I would not smoke marijuana again, that this was the last time. (It wasn't easy at that time for me.) He kind of understood what I was saying, because from that day on he hasn't called me again.

Before I typed up this article, I wasn't sure I would be able to do it. I also want to thank Master Li and express my respect and support for the students who are being persecuted in China. If it were not for Falun Dafa I would still be wasting my life, day after day.

A Teenager Experiences Many Benefits from Practicing Falun Dafa

By Tim Wu, Pennsylvania, U.S.A.

I am fourteen years old and going into the ninth grade this year.

My parents started practicing Falun Dafa in February of 1999. At that time, I didn't really pay attention to what they were doing. I just saw that they were doing a very gentle, slow-moving exercise every day. However, after just a couple of weeks, I couldn't avoid noticing the changes in my family. My mom used to have problems sleeping at night, usually not falling asleep easily. But I noticed that she started sleeping very well, and looked energetic. My dad seemed to be not getting angry or raising his voice at me easily. With these incredible things happening around me, I couldn't help mimicking the movements of their exercises to see what would happen to me. After doing the movements for a little while, my body became really warm and the exercises felt very soothing. My hands were especially warm. I didn't know how this slow-moving exercise got my whole body warm so easily, because when I run and jump while playing basketball, I still can rarely get warm at all. It was amazing.

I liked to do the movements very much. Not long after I learned the exercises, I was able to do the double lotus sitting meditation for over fifty minutes. Although it was sometimes uncomfortable, it felt good to do it.

Later, I went to group practice sites with my parents sometimes, and I noticed that all the practitioners were very friendly. I didn't know why they were all so nice, so I asked my parents. They told me that the movements were just one part of Falun Gong. The other part was to practice the central components of Falun Gong, which were the principles of Truthfulness, Compassion, and Forbearance. My mom handed me a book called *Zhuan Falun* and said, "This book will answer any questions you have." I wanted to start reading, so I joined my parents as they read the book in the evening. We read together in a group, taking turns reading. They read the Chinese version, and I read the English version. After reading the whole book once, I still had many things I didn't understand, but what I did understand was that Master Li wants us to be good people and get rid of various negative behaviors and thoughts.

After learning Falun Gong, I feel it has benefited my life very much. My health has improved. My friends in school are always getting sick and having to stay home sometimes, like I used to, as well. But I have not gotten sick for a long time. I had perfect attendance all this year and last year. My studies in school have improved too. I am now in all honors classes and have straight A's. Also, when I first started reading *Zhuan Falun*, I could only read the English version. When I tried to read the Chinese, I didn't know many of the words and I always messed up. I didn't understand what I read, either. So I often got very frustrated from that. But my parents often encouraged me with what Master Li said in *Zhuan Falun*, "When it's difficult to endure, you can endure it. When it's impossible to do, you can do it." So I followed these words and just kept reading. I read just about every day now, and I can read the whole book in Chinese slowly without too many mistakes.

Falun Gong has also improved my character. Teacher has said, "You should always be benevolent and kind to others, and consider others when doing anything." (*Zhuan Falun*) . I have tried to be kind to my classmates, never getting into fights or arguments like I used to. For example, one time, my friend accidentally spilled soda on my binder and got all the papers wet. Before studying Falun Gong, I would have been really mad. Instead, I held it in this time. I just thought that he did not spill the soda on purpose, and there was not really any reason to get mad at him. So my friend said he was sorry and he helped me clean it up. I am happy that I didn't get angry with him. Otherwise, he would have gotten angry with me too, and there would have been a big argument.

In July of 1999, probably because they thought there were too many people practicing Falun Dafa, the Chinese Communist regime banned it. From then on, just because Dafa practitioners persisted in practicing Falun Dafa, many of them were sent to labor camps, prisons, and even mental hospitals [as a way to discredit and persecute them]. Thousands and thousands of Falun Dafa practitioners have been brutally persecuted, and many tortured to death. I really don't understand why the Chinese Communist Party would persecute good people, and why they would be so scared of good people. As the rulers of a big country, why do they spread lies and rumors to the whole world to slander Falun Dafa? As a practitioner of Falun Dafa, I want to tell people that Falun Dafa is good, and expose the wicked acts of Jiang Zemin and his followers, who confuse right and wrong and fiercely persecute Falun Dafa. I should safeguard Dafa. In the past couple of years, I've had various opportunities to do this.

I have a Chinese friend who has a Chinese satellite dish at his home, so he often watches news reports regarding Falun Gong made by the Chinese regime. One time, he told me some things defaming Falun Gong, and also asked me why I practiced. I responded to him by saying: "How would you know the truth about these things? Why do you believe those lies of the Chinese Communist Party? Have you read the book *Zhuan Falun*?" From then on, he never brought up Falun Gong again. But in my heart, I wish that he would read *Zhuan Falun* sometime.

Putting "Truthfulness, Compassion, Forbearance" To Work In My Daily Life

By Diego Manca, Italy

I am a Falun Dafa practitioner from Italy. I'm 52 years old.

About two years ago I had the good fortune to become familiar with Falun Dafa, and since then the quality of my life has changed tremendously. Back then, I was having a hard time. I was fifty, and I had just lost my job and was searching for a new one. At home, my wife and I didn't understand each other. She is my partner and a good mother to our daughter. However, we quarreled every day and I was very upset.

One day, a friend of mine came to visit me because she needed to send an email from my computer. She is a Tai Chi and Yoga teacher and she asked me if I had heard about Falun Gong. I answered that I had read about it in the newspapers (it was September 1999) but I did not exactly know what it was. So I searched on the Internet for related information and found many links. Being curious, I downloaded the book *Falun Gong.* After reading it, I was really anxious to read other practitioners' experiences. I was really shocked because everything was for free: the teachings, the books, the videos, and the music. I honestly could not believe it and thought that it was a trick to make money. However, reading hundreds of practitioners' experiences, little by little, I became convinced that Falun Dafa must be something really worthwhile. What I was interested in was not the fact that as a practitioner, I could have some particular powers, but the fact of putting the three principles of "Truthfulness, Compassion and Forbearance" to work in my daily life. From this I believed I would become a better person and improve the quality of life for both myself and the people around me.

From then on I started putting into practice the first principle, Truthfulness, in the sense that I did not want to lie any more. I thought it would be easy, but it wasn't at all. I used to tell lies to myself and to others; now I gradually became aware of them. I am learning to tell the truth. I noticed that by just applying these principles in my life, I have more energy. I think that all the energy I previously used to construct the castles of my lies can be saved, and I feel the joy of liberating this energy.

I understand the second principle, Compassion, as being kind to the people I see every day in my family, at work, on the bus, etc. I think I was always a kind person, but now it is different: I think that we are, as human beings, one entity— kind to ourselves when we are kind to others. I hope that this thought is not too selfish.

I notice that behaving in this way—not lying, being kind, being tolerant and having patience, trying to behave in a noble way, my life has become more beautiful and full of joy. Many people around me regard Falun Gong as a very good thing. I never tried to convince them of how good our cultivation practice is; all I did was prove it by my actions. Of course it is very, very difficult. Many times, in the family and at work, I am still not able to behave exactly as a true practitioner, but I am learning and improving.

My job appears now to be a very fertile environment for upgrading my character. It is at work that I learned to be a good cultivator and do a good job simultaneously. My work and my family changed, and I think that they all prefer me as a cultivator to the person I was in the past. When I first started practicing, my wife was very unhappy with my practice. However, she changed her mind when she saw my transformation.

As a practitioner, I treat all my problems as tests to improve myself and become a better person. I have started a journey and have found that at the beginning of my journey my biggest obstacle is myself. I will make it though, through persistent practice and special attention to upgrading my character.

I am very grateful for what I have received from Falun Dafa. If this is the highest level that I reach in my cultivation (I am sure it is not), I would still find it the most worthwhile endeavor of my life. It has made me a better person, given me a righteous path to follow and a way to make sense of the circumstances that surround me. It has provided me with a more civilized way to react—more civilized than in the past, when I would usually, with my ordinary mentality, react with hurt or frustration, or more likely, anger.

Up to now, all the problems and questions that I have come across through my cultivation were answered through reading the book *Zhuan Falun* and Master Li's articles. I also believe that the problems I will meet later on can also be answered in this way.

I want to add one last thing. I think that as practitioners, we must use our wisdom to clarify the truth to the people and spread Dafa. I am a writer and I think that if I can touch the hearts of the people in my work, it is because the readers can find "Truthfulness, Compassion, Forbearance" between the lines.

Walking an Upright Path and Starting a New Life

By a practitioner in China

I am a 24-year-old man who once lost his way. I was lucky to learn about Falun Dafa when I was released from the forced labor camp last May. I was awakened, convinced, and determined to cultivate myself following the guidance of Falun Dafa. It has been over five months now and I have changed into a completely different person and found my way again.

I remember at the labor camp, despite the hard work that was imposed on me, my heart remained wild, even though I agreed to be a different person when released. I thought I would not take part in any illegal activities anymore, but, rather, devote myself to making more money and compensating for my lost youth. My brain was full of ideas on how to make a fortune.

But my heart was in great pain after I read Master Li's books on Falun Dafa. I regretted all the bad things I did and all the karma that I added to myself daily. I realized that I was going against the fundamental principles of the universe: Truthfulness, Compassion, Forbearance. My family and friends were trying to make me a better person, but I did not respond to positive incentives and thought being a bad person would be more beneficial. Consequently, I never wanted to be good. Master Li reveals the reasons why one should be a good person by discussing the universal principles, human nature, moral standards, and the development of human society. It made me realize what kind of a person one wants to become is a crucial issue with respect to whether or not one can improve. I am determined to be a Falun Gong practitioner, to be a good person, to assimilate to Truthfulness, Compassion, Forbearance, and to return to my true nature.

The difficulties in cultivation, however, come from many directions. The first conflicts often come from one's own family. I am a young man, but it was very difficult for me to find work since I am only a middle school graduate and the labor camp sentence did not help either. Nobody in my family liked the fact that I stayed at home and did not work. In addition, I read Master Li's book and also did the exercises at home, which my family members could neither understand nor accept. I was always being berated for no reason. I treated these incidents as obstacles that I had to overcome and opportunities for me to improve my character. I set out to be a good son at home and a good person in society. No matter how badly other people treated me, I always looked into my own heart to find my shortcomings, measured all things using the standards of Dafa, and acted accordingly.

After I started cultivation, I volunteered to do all the housework and cultivated my character through studying the Fa. I gradually got rid of many bad habits that I could not previously give up. Nowadays my family is much more pleasant. Even though I still have many things that need to be improved, I have changed a great deal from inside and have become a better person. I am also more energetic.

There is one more story I would like to share. There was a big flood last year in my hometown in July. My family was remodeling our house, and we had bought some sand and placed it downstairs. After the flood, some people who lived nearby came over, planning to steal the sand. My dad tried to stop them but nobody listened. When I found out, I rushed down to stop them before giving any thought to the matter. Even though the whole thing did not escalate, I did say some bad things such as, "I am not afraid of death" to scare them off. They all knew my past and did not dare to proceed. I regretted my behavior a great deal after this incident, as my competitive nature was revealed. I realized that I did not pass this test. Of course, I did not yell or hit people like I would have before. If it had been the old me, I would have beaten them up if I was taken advantage of, not to mention stealing sand from my house.

In the past, people who lived in our building were afraid of me and also hated me. They often rolled their eyes and gave me dirty looks. When I was sent to the labor camp, everybody smiled and felt relieved. When I came back, they all thought that the troublemaker had returned and disasters were going to happen. Their opinions completely changed after I started cultivation in Falun Dafa. Then, during the flood, I voluntarily built a boat and traveled two miles with a few other young men to obtain clean water for everybody to use. The sun was baking hot and the water was cold and dirty. The ground was burning hot and my feet blistered, but I did not complain. I thought, "I am a practitioner of Falun Dafa, and this is something I ought to do." I also helped people from other buildings move. I swam out to buy food and drinks for everybody. Actions speak louder than words. Everybody complemented me and smiled.

Of course, making people treat me nicely was not my intention. Cultivation in Falun Dafa, however, has generated this positive effect. I would not have acted this way if it were not for Falun Dafa. Indeed I have changed. My character has improved. I am more determined to cultivate. No matter what obstacles I encounter in the future, I will use Falun Dafa as my mirror and teacher to discipline myself and upgrade my entire being. I will reach the criteria of a true Falun Dafa practitioner, be a good person, and make positive contributions to society.

Why I Chose to Practice Falun Dafa: The Experience of a Doctor of Western and Chinese Medicine and Former Researcher of Qigong and Acupuncture

By Shao Xiaodong, Japan

I obtained my bachelor's degree from China's Western Medical Science University and my master's degree from the Chinese Medical Science Research Institute. I have a master's degree in Qigong and Acupuncture certified by the State Education Commission of China, and have served as the Deputy Chairman of the Heilongjiang Provincial Qigong Science Research Society and counselor to the Liaoning Provincial Qigong Science Research Society. I was also nominated and recommended by Mr. Zhang Zhenhuan, formerly Director of China National Defense Science and Industry Commission and now Chairman of the China Qigong Science Research Society and China Human Body Science Society, as academic counselor of therapeutic Qigong. Since 1985, I have had many opportunities to give lectures in European and American cities by invitation.

In 1989, I came to Japan to teach. In 1990, I accepted an appointment to work in Japan and settled down in Tokyo. Prior to coming to Japan, I worked as a leading attending physician for China's State Chinese Medical Science Research Institute in Beijing and a Specially Invited Lecturer for the Therapeutic Qigong Research Institute of the Beijing Chinese Medical Science and Medicine University.

To a Falun Dafa practitioner, the education, degrees and titles mentioned above are of little significance. I list them here just to show that I have received formal training in modern science and I am not a novice at Chinese and Western medical sciences, qigong and human body science research. In addition, being a senior high school graduate in the early 1960's and having gone through the Cultural Revolution and all types of ideological movements, I am used to evaluating various theories and doctrines with a critical eye. I would not carelessly believe in or blindly follow anyone or any theory. As to things new to mankind, I am of the opinion that we should not carelessly believe them, or carelessly deny them. Rather, we should avoid the influence of our acquired perceptions and probe them with rational thinking and personal experience. Only after that shall we be able to draw a conclusion.

Today I will talk about my personal experience in choosing to practice Falun Dafa. What I will talk about here is from a beginner's perspective, and won't be of much help to veteran practitioners. But to beginning practitioners and those interested in learning Falun Dafa, it may help them learn more about Falun Dafa and start the practice.

In mid-1993, I left Japan for China to conduct research on various schools of qigong practices. Near the Golden

Fish Pond in Zhongshan Park in Beijing, I heard pleasant music and became curious about the source. I saw dozens of people practicing a qigong system that I had never seen before.

After the practice finished, I had a conversation with the practitioners. They told me that the practice was called Falun Gong and the teacher was Mr. Li Hongzhi. They also mentioned that Falun Gong was a cultivation practice and Master Li not only taught the practice, but also lectured on the Fa (law and principles), which guide spiritual cultivation at a high level. I thought to myself: this might be the advanced cultivation Dafa (Great Way) I have been seeking for years. Then, I started learning Falun Gong in the park every morning. Upon hearing that Master Li was going to give another series of lectures in Beijing, I asked the contact person of that practice site to enter my name too.

August 27, 1993 was a day most worthy of celebration in my life. On that day I became a practitioner at the 13th Falun Gong lecture series in Beijing.

During that period, every evening I went to attend the lectures given by Master Li at the No. 27 Beijing Locomotive Factory way outside the city proper. Returning home after the 3rd lecture, I practiced the fifth set of exercises for 30 minutes and felt light and comfortable all over my body, with no numbness or pain when doing the cross-legged meditation. That was the first time I physically experienced the great power of Falun Dafa. Before I attended the lectures, when I practiced lotus sitting for up to 30 minutes, I would feel swelling pains. In the past, I had been involved in human body supernormal capability research conducted by China's science and technology communities. In those days, the *People's Daily* (the official newspaper of the Chinese Communist Party) published a commentator's article denying the existence of human supernormal capabilities. At the same time some people in the literature and science circles also published articles in central and local government newspapers and magazines to attack qigong, labeling human body supernormal capabilities as pseudo-science, ignorance and superstition. The overall situation turned ominous under the circumstances. As a result, many people who had come to probe supernormal capabilities were scared away, and only a few serious scientists continued their research.

At that time, under the sponsorship of the renowned scientist Qian Xuesen, we called together people with supernormal capabilities from across the country. With the coordinated effort of researchers from the Physics Research Institute, the High Energy Physics Institute and the Biophysics Institute of the Chinese Academy of Science and the No.1129 Institute of the Public Security Ministry, we made use of such hi-tech instruments as micro-beam video cameras, reaction testers and brain electroscopes and testified to the validity of human body supernormal capabilities, including capabilities of peering through objects with the celestial eye, clairvoyance and moving objects through dimensional barriers. Therefore, we came to conclude that besides the existing physical dimension we live in, there also exist other dimensions. The human body experiments conducted by China's upper-level science circles at that time also confirmed the existence of other dimensions, which were called by the researchers "hidden states" or "field states". Later on, with the help of high-speed cameras, researchers from the National Defense Science and Industry Commission even succeeded in capturing tablets of medicine passing through the dimensional barriers of a glass bottle under the energy effect of supernormal capabilities. It was because of this series of successful experiments in the human body sciences that the Central Committee of the Communist Party and the State Council at that time formulated the "Three Nos" policy regarding human body science and qigong (that is, No Promoting, No Criticizing, No Debating). However, since 1996 some Chinese media, including the Guangming Daily, violated the central government's "Three Nos" policy by openly attacking Falun Gong. The situation later escalated to the public security bureau arresting Falun Gong practitioners in Tianjin and the April 25, 1999 peaceful appeal in Beijing.

In the recent anti-Falun Gong campaign waged by the Chinese regime, a few so-called experts or scholars have relied on the limited knowledge and assumptions of today's human sciences to rashly deny phenomena yet unknown to them. Their attitude of jumping to conclusions subjectively itself is unscientific and unsupported. Even from the perspective of experimental science, we should not recklessly negate things that we cannot understand temporarily.

In this article, I have talked about things related to empirical sciences and cultivation theories that are often very close to theories in human society, in hopes of having society understand us, or at least to avoid some misconceptions. It is also our wish that the Chinese regime and its top leaders will clarify their misunderstandings of Falun Dafa and its kindhearted practitioners.

Personally, I like to practice cultivation alone quietly and enjoy the peace. However, when Falun Gong is being mistreated like this, as a veteran practitioner, I have the obligation to stand up to clarify some facts and reveal the truth.

Recently, the *People's Daily* carried a commentator's article accusing Falun Gong of "amassing wealth". That is totally groundless. For the 10-day Falun Gong teaching series given by Master Li in Beijing that I attended, I only paid 40 yuan, the equivalent of 500 Japanese Yen (or $5), which was the lowest charge I have ever known for qigong teaching sessions in China. Even now I still have the Completion Certificate issued at that time, with the cover signed by the China Qigong Research Society. It was the China Qigong Research Society that had organized the event. At the Falun Gong practice sites I had visited in several parks of Beijing, all of the Falun Gong classes were free of charge and given by volunteers. Furthermore, the Beijing Assistance Center did not even have an office. I personally had offered to make a donation to Falun Gong, but the Falun Gong Research Society graciously declined my request after asking Master Li. According to the staff of the Research Society, Master Li said that no individual donations would be accepted, because after affluent practitioners made a donation, the less well-off practitioners might also want to make a donation. However, their financial inability would make them feel bad. That's why no individual donations were accepted. I was deeply moved by the reply. This was real, selfless benevolence and compassion! I also knew that the contact person of the Dalian Assistance Center had purchased a villa in her personal capacity and wanted to give it to Master Li as a gift. But Master Li did not accept the gift. I had also proposed to donate the 6 suites of real estate investment I purchased in Beijing to Falun Gong, but Master Li rejected my proposal again. All the above facts are what I have personally seen or heard.

Since 1995, the Public Security Ministry has carried out two nation-wide investigations into Falun Gong and concluded that Falun Gong had no political background and should be regulated as per the Regular Public Group Security Rules. In fact, Falun Gong teaches good citizenship and offers instructions to genuine practitioners in cultivation practice. It brings only benefits and no harm to society. In short, the accusations made by the Chinese Communist Party against Falun Gong are non-factual. We believe that history will give a fair judgment on Falun Gong.

"Truthfulness, Compassion, Forbearance," Even While Driving a Car

By a European practitioner

I climbed into my car. My rear window was adorned with the words: "Truthfulness, Compassion, Forbearance." I was in a hurry, so I stepped on the gas pedal harder. I overtook a taxi and another vehicle, not even realizing that I was driving in an erratic manner. When I stopped at a traffic light, another car approached slowly, pulled up beside me and stopped. The driver rolled down his window and said to me, "It would be great if you would drive according to the words on the sticker in your rear window."

This made me realize what a huge responsibility it is to drive through a city with those three words on my car, to live each second according to those three words. I must not ignore them when I sit behind the wheel.

I thanked the driver and promised to mend my ways.

Since then I have been driving more carefully and obeying all the traffic rules. I have to live with "Truthfulness, Compassion, Forbearance," not only when I am behind the wheel, but also when speaking and in my other daily routines. Those three words are becoming more and more important.

How Falun Dafa Changed a Former Thief

By a practitioner in Liaoning Province, China

I am 30 years old. I am from Jinzhou City in Liaoning Province. I am now detained in a forced labor camp in Jinzhou City because of theft.

I have a dark history. I left school when I was only 10 years old. I was sent to the City Labor School because of theft when I was 15 years old. Two years later, I was given a sentence of 1.5 years in prison as a thief. When I was 19 years old, I was given a sentence of 10 years in prison, again because of stealing. I was released in 1996. In 1999, I was given a detention of 15 days for stealing and I escaped through a window. Ten days later, I was caught and taken back to the detention center and detained together with some Falun Gong practitioners.

At that time, the Chinese Communist regime was attacking Falun Gong madly on TV and in the newspapers, claiming that Falun Gong was harmful to people. Therefore, I was very curious about Falun Gong practitioners, and I wanted to know how bad they were and whether they were even worse than me. However, the truth was beyond my expectation. They were from all walks of life. There were workers, farmers, officials, and doctors. They were detained because they had gone to Beijing to appeal for Falun Gong or practiced their exercises in the parks. They did not look down upon me just because I was a convicted thief. Instead, they told me to be a good person and not to steal and not to do bad things anymore. I was deeply touched by their words. In particular, some of them had no hatred or complaints when they were being cursed at or beaten up by the guards. They always treated those guards kindly and told them about the principles of becoming a good person. I was very surprised and also perplexed. The TV programs had been saying how bad Falun Gong was. Then how come so many people had become so good after learning Falun Gong? I had to admit that they were really good people from what I saw.

I suddenly felt very regretful that in the past ten years I had committed so many bad deeds. How wonderful it would be if I could be a good person like these Falun Gong practitioners! Then I told my thoughts to Yan Li, Li Huan-bao, Liu Wan-sheng and other practitioners in my cell. They gave me a copy of *Zhuan Falun* (the main text of Falun Gong). I finished reading it with great eagerness. Then, I had a sleepless night. My past life as a thief for a dozen years appeared in my mind. I had done so many bad things.

I remembered that my neighbors had praised me as a kind child. However, when I grew up, all kinds of bad thoughts in society and the desire for money started to pollute me and control me and push me into the abyss. In prison, I had been educated about the laws. Some of the better guards had also tried to help me to change. However, these were all useless to me. Those evil thoughts still controlled me and I could not free myself from doing bad things. After finishing reading *Zhuan Falun*, I understood that laws and policies in human society could only change someone on the surface, and that only a higher law could change someone's heart and make one become genuinely good. I was really lucky to be able to learn Falun Dafa in prison. I decided to be a good person from then on.

Later, I was sent to a labor camp in Jinzhou City. I was worried very much that I might not be able to meet other practitioners because I still wanted to ask them many questions. Surprisingly, however, I met many other practitioners there! I suddenly realized that Falun Dafa would shed light into every corner of the world.

When my family members came to visit me, they became very angry after they learned that I had started to practice Falun Gong. They said, "How come you learned Falun Gong here? Right now the whole country is attacking Falun Gong!" I told them, "You do not understand the truth. Falun Gong is not like what is said on TV and in the newspapers. Falun Gong teaches people to become good people and is wonderful." However, they didn't want to listen to me. They even threatened that they would not visit me again if I continued to practice Falun Gong. I started shedding tears on the spot. However, I realized immediately that it was a test for me. I would become a good person by learning Falun Gong and in the future my family members would then know that Falun Gong is indeed good.

I have studied Falun Dafa now for three months. The guards and criminals in the detention center and labor camp all know that Falun Dafa practitioners are good people.

Anesthetist Refuses to Accept "Extra Income" and Kickbacks after Practicing Falun Gong

By a practitioner in China

In Mainland China, if you go to the hospital for an operation, there are usually two people to whom you must give extra money in red envelopes. One is the surgeon who will perform the operation, and the other is the anesthetist. It's not clear when this practice began, but quite often the money in the red envelopes is their main source of income. Though the amount of money in the red envelope varies from person to person, according to my younger sister who works as an anesthetist in the hospital, an ordinary anesthetist like her would receive between seven or eight thousand to ten thousand *yuan* per month [500 *yuan* is the average monthly salary for an urban worker in China]. In contrast, a doctor's monthly salary is about one to two thousand *yuan*. Another source of extra income is kickbacks from drug companies for prescribing expensive medicine. Though it cannot be compared to the amount of money in red envelopes, it is also quite sizable.

After practicing Falun Gong, my younger sister, who is an anesthetist working in a hospital, stopped taking the red envelopes and kickbacks for prescribing certain drugs.

My younger sister began her practice relatively late. Before the persecution began in 1999, her mother-in-law practiced Falun Gong, and her father-in-law also practiced for a while. However at that time, she did not know much about Falun Gong, and took it as just an exercise for healing illness and keeping fit. After July 20, 1999, her mother-in-law gave up practicing Falun Gong under the overwhelming pressure from the Chinese Communist Party. My sister tried her best to persuade her mother-in-law, saying, "Mom, if you feel it is good, then you should keep practicing it. Why should you care about what the media says? I feel it is good for you to practice this qigong because it has made you healthy." However, this elderly lady had experienced political movements such as the Cultural Revolution before and was scared to death. She did not dare to continue to practice.

At one point, I learned from my younger sister that she was disappointed with the deterioration of morality in society, the coldness between human beings, and people's efforts to take advantage of others. She felt puzzled over human existence. She felt really empty, lonely and depressed. She even felt despair for the future.

I talked to her over the phone about Falun Dafa, and soon she began to practice. Two days later, I received a phone call. She said, "Hello, elder sister, I have read *Zhuan Falun*." I asked, "How do you feel?" She replied, "It is so great! I have decided not to take money in the red envelopes any more!" Her voice was full of excitement. "Is that true? You are so quick to improve your character!" I was so happy from the bottom of my heart.

Immediately, she continued to talk in a flow of eloquence. She said she finally understood the meaning of life, understood why human beings were living in this world, and also understood the value of life. She said she did not feel confused any more. After a period of time, she told me over the phone that ever since she cultivated Dafa, she felt a completely new sense of enrichment and tranquility in her soul. She did not feel anxious, empty, or depressed any more. She also felt that she received a new strength for actively moving ahead in life, and had found a new meaning to her life.

Later on, all kinds of propaganda attacking Dafa came out, becoming more and more irresponsible, slanderous and deceptive. China was a truly terrifying environment. Facing all of this, I was put in a state of confusion. Every day, my mind was full of thoughts about current events, and I did not have the presence of mind to see how she was doing. For a long period of time, she also had similar problems. Occasionally, she called to tell me about how she felt. I learned that she did not have a very good state of mind. She did not study the Falun Gong teachings for a long period of time, and neither did she practice the exercises. She was agonized and could not understand why such a good practice would be subjected to defamation and attack! She could not believe how the CCP leader, Jiang Zemin, in order to persecute a group of good people, could disregard the facts and make up all kinds of lies to deceive the people. She started to jog early in the morning. However, every morning, she heard people talking about Falun Gong in the park. Some elderly ladies sighed, looking at the garbage on the ground: "When the Falun Gong practitioners practiced the exercises here, it was so clean. You see how dirty it is now."

During that period of time, though my younger sister stopped studying the Fa and doing the exercises, she never forgot about the principles she learned. She refused to collect any money in the red envelopes from the patients and did not accept any kickbacks.

After I thought about the current situation, I decided to renew my practice and help my younger sister to come back also. Since she cultivated her inner self seriously and made efforts in upgrading her character, she made very quick progress. When she met patients who did not feel comfortable when she refused their money, she would take the money first and after the operation, she would return the money to them. In her work, she didn't complain about her assignments, jockey for position with others, or worry about personal gain and loss. She gained the respect of her peers, and used her wisdom to clarify the truth to her patients and colleagues.

"I Can Hardly Believe the Person I Used To Be"

By Trish Brady, Texas, U.S.A.

At the young age of seven I started reading books about everything I could about the universe and our solar system. I read the Bible through and through and felt close to God, and I knew deep within that I must become a better person. At eight years old I stepped forward in church and received Baptism. Still I felt there was something more, something I needed to do, but what it was exactly, I did not know.

As I grew up, my family split apart, and eventually my parents divorced. I fell away from Christianity and started going along with mainstream society and materialism. I am from eastern Kentucky and have only a ninth grade education due to a rebellious and angry temperament. I always blamed my parents for all my downfalls and tribulations. I tumbled and lost myself in self-pity and negative associations. My teenage years were chaotic at best, but inside I still had a little divine nature left.

At 20 I joined an ancient mystical society and through its teaching learned many things about the world and felt better grounded. I belonged to this mystical society for many years, but it did not keep me from sliding down even further, and it never emphasized virtue or how to be a better person. While still clinging to it for protection, I continued my search to find the truth, but everywhere I looked it was not there. Once I felt drawn toward learning something about eastern thought and read a book on Zen Buddhism. As I read, I came to a part that talked about meditating and sitting in silence and enlightening on your own. I remember my frustration with what I read and thinking, "Enlighten to what?" I put the book down and sadly never picked up any other books of eastern thought again because I figured that I could not understand them.

By the age of 28 I was developing severe allergies and chronic bronchitis, which led me to the hospital, sometimes three times a year, with pneumonia. I was still a member of the secret order, the ancient mystical society I spoke of earlier, yet my life had become deplorable. I was depressed and lost. I gave up on finding the way and plunged full force into the big dye vat of society.

By this time I had three children. My family life was very strained. I was not an ideal mother. I always lost my temper and always thought of myself first before anyone else. If anyone wronged me, I would surely wrong them much worse to get back at them. I had many enemies. I had an affair to get back at my husband's having an affair, and our marriage never fully recovered.

My mother had lived in Saudi Arabia for many years and never knew her grandchildren. She moved back to the US in 1998. She moved to Texas and asked me to move there with her. It took two years for me to agree because my relationship with my mother had always been rocky in the past.

We moved in with my mother in July of 2000. My husband and I thought we were leaving our problems behind. We got good jobs working in the telecommunications industry. By September we moved out and got our own place. Then suddenly everyone was laid off and we lost our jobs. We moved back in with my mother. Terrible fights started between my husband and me and this made things with my mother very bad. I was still involved with the secret order in Texas and would travel to Austin once a month to attend a meeting.

I became very close to the regional monitor of the group. I was looking to him to maybe answer some of the questions I had as to the truth of why was I here, but he just wanted to have a physical relationship. I totally lost faith in the order and quit. Something inside of me was waking up. I suddenly had a strange desire to learn Chinese. I started thinking about cultivation practices that I had heard about. I knew that affairs were wrong, and I wanted to be moral. I wanted to go to China and find a master to guide me! Where was I going to find one? I couldn't just leave my family and go away. I went to the highest hill in Canyon Lake and just sat there and spoke to whoever was there to possibly listen to my plea. It was a silent prayer to the universe for a way to cultivate back. Little did I know that someone was listening.

A few days later my husband, my mother, and I all got into a big argument that resulted in her throwing us all out. We had nowhere to go but to a homeless shelter. It was the best thing that ever happened to me. My husband found another job, and while he was gone from the shelter to work, the children and I would walk to the local public library. We had access to a VCR and I owned a computer but had no Internet access. We would borrow videos and books and CDs. On my second visit to the library, I came across a video entitled *The True Story of Falun Gong.* I had never heard of Falun Gong, but for some unknown reason, I borrowed it and felt an urgency to watch it.

I can remember putting it into the recorder and pressing "Play" and seeing the Falun symbol and hearing the music. It dumbfounded me. I was speechless and could think of nothing else but watching the story. In that single instant knew I had found what I had been searching for all of my life. I went back to the library the next day to use their computer and look up www.falundafa.org. I downloaded each exercise onto a disk, took it back to the shelter, put it into my computer, practiced the movements, and read the book.

Searching the www.falundafa.org website, I found a group practice site in my area and went there for the first time and met several practitioners. I finally purchased a copy of *Zhuan Falun* and went home and read it all in one day.

My husband and I started looking at houses so that we could move out of the shelter. One evening we went to look at a house. We stopped by a gas station to fill up our car and get something to drink. As I was coming out of the store and walking toward the car, a girl I never met before walked up to me and asked me to open my hand. She seemed harmless, so I obliged and she put a huge bug into my hand. I screamed and she started to laugh. The bug flew up into the air and landed on the sidewalk. I picked it up as she went into the store. I looked at it and realized it was one of those fake, trick bugs, and this made me furious. I got into the car, waiting for my husband to get back in with the kids, and I was thinking to myself, "I must forbear. Isn't this the kind of thing Master Li talks about in the book?" I was still so angry. How dare that girl do that to me? I yelled at her as we drove away and I failed my first big test. I felt very bad afterward.

A week later we moved into that house and I continued to go to group practice and study the teachings of Falun Gong. Every day after I came home from the practice, I would sleep for a long time and have loose stools. My body was being cleansed. I coughed up stuff out of my lungs, but I noticed I no longer needed my rescue inhaler and I bravely quit taking the antihistamine medication for a day to see what would happen. I had taken it for ten years and could not breathe well without it. I also had a nebulizer because sometimes I had to have a deep treatment for my lungs. I went off of it and, to my surprise, I didn't need it anymore! I quit taking everything. My allergies all went away. I am still practicing to this day. Falun Dafa totally changed my life, and I am a different person now. I can hardly believe the person I used to be. I owe my good health and all the positive things in my life to Falun Dafa.

My Experience Working in a Chinese Restaurant

By a Chinese student in the U.S.A.

I started working in a Chinese restaurant at the beginning of the year 2000. There were all kinds of people with different backgrounds there. One of my classmates who was familiar with the people working in this restaurant told me in advance about who was a thief, who I needed to be wary of and so forth. I thought this would be of no concern for a genuine Falun Dafa practitioner who could easily handle it. What I could do was to change the environment around me.

The workers in the restaurant usually rested right after they finished their duties, never thinking of helping others. When I started working there, I helped others every day. They asked me why I did this. I told them that I practiced Falun Dafa and learned from Dafa that I should consider others first in any situation. They were surprised and deeply moved. Since then, the practice of specifying duties to each helper in the restaurant has stopped because of the harmonious relationship among the employees and the fact that everybody is willing to help others. Conflicts between co-workers have also become fewer and fewer.

Some Chinese workers at the restaurant who had recently arrived in America could not drive, so I drove them to work and back home every day. Some colleagues tried to persuade me not to do such a "stupid" thing. I said, "If they didn't do this to earn a living, nobody would do these heavy and dirty jobs. We can't just think of ourselves all the time. We also need to consider others." After this conversation, my co-workers kept silent.

A customer who frequently visited our restaurant never left tips. As a result, neither the manager nor the employees were friendly towards him. But I treated him the same way as I treated the other customers. Surprisingly, he gave me a two-dollar tip. All of my colleagues were stunned. I told them, "Everyone has a compassionate mind. If we did not think of getting as much money as possible from the customer's pocket, the situation would change." My colleagues' minds became less occupied with money since then and business in the restaurant got better. The manager said that I brought good fortune to the restaurant.

Whenever I had a chance, I would introduce Dafa and clarify the truth of Dafa to them. A 40-year-old man who used to be a department director of a university in Shanghai had to work in this restaurant because he could not find another job due to his poor English. Nobody talked with him because they suspected that he was not a good person. I thought I should be responsible for everybody around me, so I introduced Dafa to him. To my surprise, he was immediately interested in knowing the truth of Falun Dafa. I gave him a Dafa book, and since then, I noticed that he has turned out to be a generous person.

Three months later, my husband found a job with good pay, so I did not have to work in that restaurant anymore. Everybody was very sad when I left. They said they would like to work with me if I would run a restaurant someday. The manager and his wife also told me that they would help me whenever I needed it. The chef, whom I had barely talked with, said, "I have worked here for more than ten years, but I have never met such a kind and good person like you."

I used to be very sensitive about my reputation. If I did not practice Falun Dafa, I would not have accepted a waitress job in a restaurant without complaining. Because of Dafa, I did not feel any fatigue after working hard all day. It is Falun Dafa that created a new life for me, gave me strength and helped me to discard all kinds of bad notions that are part of many people's lives.

Conflicts Lasting Decades Are Resolved after Family Practices Falun Dafa

By Hongni, Canada

My family and I were fortunate to find Falun Dafa in 2004. During the past several years, whenever I passed by Chinatown and the university, I frequently received flyers and CDs from Dafa practitioners. Although I didn't pay much attention to them, looking at the flyers and CDs, which had obviously been made with great effort, I felt that at least these Dafa practitioners were sincere and kind. I often saw them practicing and teaching the exercises in groups in the plaza and at the university. I saw with my own eyes that people who practiced Falun Gong were all very peaceful and orderly. Everybody did a lot of work quietly. After I read articles in the *The Epoch Times* newspaper about how many had become better and healthier people after they started practicing, I became curious and had a favorable opinion of Dafa. Three, four years passed. Although I missed many chances to get to know Dafa, the things that practitioners did quietly planted seeds in my mind to help my family come to Dafa later on.

Because I saw with my own eyes the practitioners'

peacefulness and their devotion to their belief, I was empathic towards Falun Gong over its being persecuted by the Chinese Communist Party (CCP) for no rational reason. Finally I really wanted to understand what kind of belief made these practitioners so persistent and why the CCP was trying everything to persecute these kind people. Just then, I remembered the Dafa website listed on the flyers. I visited http://www.falundafa.org and downloaded the online version of *Zhuan Falun*. I was deeply drawn by the wonders of the book after reading just a few pages. I felt I was on a spaceship traveling into space and exploring the profound mysteries of the universe. All of a sudden my questions about life were answered. What is good and what is evil all became clear. Black and white, truth and lies all became crystal clear.

After I was fortunate enough to become acquainted with Dafa, I didn't immediately walk onto the cultivation path. It wasn't easy for the whole family to come to practice Dafa. When I found out *Zhuan Falun* was such a good book, I urged my father to read it, hoping it could help him, an honest person with a bad temper. But my father knew my intention, and he always tried to avoid it. Winter came in no time. One day he insisted on going skating. I was a little worried, but my mother and I didn't want to stop him so we let him go. Unfortunately, we got a phone call from a hospital emergency room that my father had broken his hip and needed immediate surgery. He was almost 60 years old. It was a big shock for the family. My mother and I took good care of him, hoping he could recover quickly. But the conflicts between my mother and father persisted.

I was reading *Zhuan Falun* at the time. I understood

that only Dafa could resolve the deeply rooted conflicts in my family, so I recommended the book to my father several times. Finally my father started reading. Right away he changed. His 58 years of bad temper improved greatly. He started being tolerant, even during conflicts with my mother. His spirit improved, and all of us benefited. There were fewer conflicts in the family.

Just like that, my father started practicing. We were all so happy for him. But I, as the first person in the family who got to know Dafa, didn't continue to study and practice due to laziness. Right then, a friend that I had not seen for a long time showed up and stayed at our house for several days. Very soon we learned that she was a Dafa practitioner. With her help we learned all five exercises and together listened to Master Li's lectures on tapes.

Our whole family started practicing all five exercises. Very soon my father could stand up with the aid of a crutch. He persisted in practicing the standing exercises for two hours and the sitting exercise for one hour every day. My father's face looked younger every day. Even though he was almost 60 years old, two months after his hip fracture he could walk without assistance. We couldn't afford medical insurance because my father was on a visitor's visa. It was a miracle that he could walk on his own without a crutch. Following that, my father was able to easily pass the physical exam for a visa extension. He had to bend and raise his legs in front of the doctors. Due to this miraculous recovery after practicing Dafa, my father was able to successfully pass the physical exam.

Over the following six months my whole family practiced together. The first several months I often felt a warm stream coming down from the top of my head and spreading all over my body. I felt wonderful. Later my father went back to China, and my mother and I became lazy about practicing. I knew we shouldn't be like that and wanted to get in touch with the local practitioners so we could have a good cultivation environment to help improve ourselves. For various reasons I never got a chance to do that. Just then, a fellow practitioner we had never met called us. She called to greet my father. It turned out that my father, who likes reading *The Epoch Times*, withdrew from the CCP for our whole family after he read the *Nine Commentaries on the Communist Party*.

Later I realized that this ordinary phone call marked a huge transition in our cultivation paths. The practitioner encouraged us to participate in the group Fa study. The study site was very close to our house. At first we just thought we'd try it out, but we have not stopped going there ever since that first time. Every week we studied the Fa and shared our experiences with fellow practitioners. It became an important part of our cultivation. With encouragement and help from fellow practitioners I became very diligent in cultivation. Since then, Dafa has become part of our lives. Our whole family walked onto the cultivation path.

Over the year and a half since I began Dafa practice, we have experienced the greatness of Dafa. I had never been very healthy, even when I was very young. I had chronic tracheitis and perpetual allergic rhinitis. After I came to the West, for the first couple of years my chronic tracheitis didn't bother me much, but the perpetual allergic rhinitis gave me quite a bit of trouble. After several years I was used to having to breathe through my mouth, particularly after I started working as an information technology professional. My resistance to diseases decreased. I frequently had a cold that lingered for weeks and months. My trachea became very susceptible because I breathed through my mouth all the time. Every time I caught a cold I coughed a lot, too. Plus, I was allergic to the air conditioning and used lots of tissues. Several years ago, after riding in a car with a coworker who smoked, my chronic tracheitis came back. If I walked too fast, it was hard for me to catch my breath. I could hear the sound of my breathing through my trachea. Due to my dislike of Western medicine and treatment methods, I never took many medicines. I only took antibiotics a couple of times, but I was afraid of having to depend on them, so I ended up throwing them away. I got used to hearing the sounds from my trachea and I even didn't consider chronic tracheitis and perennial allergic rhinitis to be diseases. After I practiced Dafa for several months, I suddenly realized that all my symptoms had disappeared without my even noticing it. This was a clear case of the Fa principle of gaining naturally without pursuit.

There are so many good things about Dafa that I can't write about all of them. Dafa helped my family dispel conflicts that had existed for decades. We all benefited from it, mentally and physically. We thank Master Li, Dafa, and all Dafa practitioners who clarify the truth and spread the Fa on every street and in every corner of the world. Some have even sacrificed their lives. Their kindness has helped countless people to benefit from Falun Dafa.

Company Vice-President:
My Wonderful Experiences in the Practice of Falun Dafa

By a Western practitioner in California, U.S.A.

I work at a Silicon Valley company as vice president of marketing and sales. I'd like to share with you something truly wonderful that has impacted my life on so many positive and healthy levels.

It had been a restless night. For quite some time I had battled insomnia, had endured bouts of depression, was anxious over many issues in my life, and a lot of the time I just felt exhausted and spent. I really longed for rest and some peace and serenity in my life. I had done a lot of work on myself over the previous few years, work dealing with emotional healing and growth, spiritual reconnection, looking closely at patterns of thought, self image, behaviors, boundaries, and seeking well-being on all levels in my life. I was dealing with the breakup of a 20-year marriage and raising my daughters as we transitioned into a new way of being a family. There was great turmoil and chaos in my career because the company I had worked at for 11 years had gone into bankruptcy soon after my wife left me. My new relationship with a woman had been fraught with heartbreak and pain. I wasn't a very happy man. I knew the answers lay inside myself and I continued to search.

I awoke that morning saying I had to exercise and move my body. I had to try to break this pattern of no energy and low spirits in the morning and throughout my day. I slowly awoke, got dressed, and walked down to the park close to my house and began to walk briskly around the course. As I was walking, I glanced over to my left and saw some people doing what initially appeared to be a form of Tai Chi. As I drew closer, I saw a young Chinese woman holding her hands over her head. She warmly smiled at me and said, "Would you like to join us?" I immediately said, "Yes." There was just a knowingness that this was right.

I did the exercises and she helped me do the first two sets that I had missed. I really liked it, and she invited me back the next day at 7:00 a.m. I said, "OK." That day I noticed that I could really think clearly, and that I felt relaxed and at peace with the world. That night I slept really well. Well, all this sure got my attention, and I knew I would go back again the next morning.

Sure enough, the alarm went off at 6:15 a.m. but I was already awake, ready to embrace the day and surely the morning. I was truly excited about going again to the park to do those wonderful exercises. The volunteer assistant and the other practitioners began to lead us in the exercises. I should also mention that everybody was so warm and friendly, and their demeanor was very peaceful. We all did the five exercises, and I again felt wonderful during and after doing the exercises. I got up every day to do the exercises. I was invited to a nine-day seminar and eagerly attended. I felt so relaxed listening to the Master's words. I really liked it and felt excited to learn more and do more of this practice called Falun Gong.

Last year my girlfriend had given me a magazine article about the persecution of people in Mainland China who were doing this. Both she and I got on the Falun Gong website and downloaded informational materials. I felt an attraction to Falun Gong even then. I called one of the local numbers and the gentleman said to please come at 5:30 a.m. to a park that was far away and do this for two hours. I thought I didn't want to do that. I just wasn't ready at that time. Now I was ready and it was wonderful. I am so grateful that I made the decision to begin after the opportunity presented itself. But honestly, it wasn't really hard to decide. I just knew it was right and I really wanted to do it.

I got both the Falun Gong books and started reading, and I really liked what they had to say. The material was exciting to read and my mind felt alive and stimulated. Doing Falun Gong and studying Dafa has really had a very profound effect on my life in a very positive way. Five simple exercises and three very simple and basic principles guide my daily life. Truthfulness, Compassion, Forbearance—very simple, but very profound.

I am now much more at ease with some of the challenges I face in my life, both in my relationships and in my job. I notice I am much more relaxed and accepting while dealing with life's daily struggles. I feel like I am at home now and on the right path to truth. Truthfulness, Compassion, Forbearance. What great principles to live my life by.

Compassion and developing character are very attractive to me and enhance my life on a daily basis. I was always attracted to things that talked about coming from the heart and having compassion for all things.

When I began to practice the five Falun Gong exercises, I immediately noticed that I was calmer and more relaxed. My overall mental outlook began to really change in a very positive way. I feel that I have more clarity and mental focus.

Because Falun Gong is a very holistic practice that improves and enhances one's mental, physical, and emotional well being, I can honestly report excellent changes on both a physical and emotional level. My emotional outlook is one of feeling much more relaxed and less stressed. I feel better physically, and my energy level has increased. I am excited about embracing the day when I awake, and I sleep much better. I feel more rested and alert. Physically, I feel that a lot of the stress that I normally carry in my body has been released. My neck and shoulders are less tense and I generally feel a lot more flexible and loose.

In general my life is much more peaceful, and things that used to cause me anxiety and worry just don't seem to have such a strong effect on me now. When doing the exercises, it feels good to relax and quiet my mind and thoughts. I am very happy to be meeting new people and practitioners every week. Every practitioner I have met is a person of strong moral character and is thoughtful and considerate of everyone he or she comes into contact with. I have felt very welcomed by all that I have met. I have always been greeted with a warm smile and encouragement to continue to practice Falun Gong.

Mr. Li Hongzhi, the founder and teacher of Falun Gong, has had a very significant impact on a worldwide level, including on a growing number of practitioners here in the United States, in improving how people relate to each other and live together. The improvement of character and integrity, the development of compassion and consideration for others, and the values of honesty and truthfulness are very sound principles for us all to incorporate into our personal and professional lives.

Why are more and more people attracted to the practice of Falun Gong? Why was I attracted to it? For all of the reasons that I have mentioned above. Physically, emotionally, and intellectually, I have directly and almost immediately experienced the very positive ways that Falun Gong has enhanced my daily life. I am most thankful that I have learned of Falun Gong, and I am most eager and excited to continue on a daily basis learning more and practicing more.

I really love Falun Gong. I love doing the exercises every day, going to the discussion group once a week to read and discuss the writings of Master Li, and the wonderful people and practitioners I have met as a result of becoming involved in Falun Dafa. My mental clarity and focus have improved. My emotional well-being, spiritual connectedness, sense of acceptance, and forbearance to deal with life's challenges have all improved. I know I am on the right path of spiritual enlightenment and that in itself brings me peace and serenity. I am very grateful to have had Falun Dafa come into my life. My life is truly enhanced by my practice of it and the truly wonderful people I have met who practice Falun Gong. My cultivation energy increases each day and my character continues to develop and grow. I am a better man and a better person as a result of this cultivation practice.

Practicing Falun Dafa and Becoming a Better Person

By a Western practitioner in the U.S.A.

One day I came across Falun Gong while I was surfing the web. I had read about the persecution in China and wanted to find out what was so powerful about this spiritual practice that people in China were willing to risk their lives to clarify the truth and to exercise their right to their beliefs. I was curious to find out more, and found information about a local practice site on the Internet. When I went there, I saw people meditating in full lotus. I was struck by their peacefulness and the power of the exercises. I knew immediately that this was for me and wanted to know more about it. I attended a nine-day seminar—a videotaped lecture series given by the teacher and founder, Master Li Hongzhi. During the seminar, I knew in my heart that this practice would teach me how to be a better person.

I used to have a problem with gambling. Falun Gong showed me how to cultivate my heart and mind to assimilate into the universal principles of Truthfulness, Compassion, and Forbearance. The teachings provided the guidance I had been lacking. I immediately stopped gambling.

My wife saw remarkable changes in me in just a few months of practicing Falun Gong. She was so impressed that she started practicing too. My daughter was also struck by the changes in me and wanted to know what had brought about this transformation, so I introduced her to *Zhuan Falun*, the principal book of Master Li Hongzhi. Reading *Zhuan Falun* with her was one of the best experiences of my life.

Many of you have seen practitioners doing the exercises. Maybe you've also been struck by the beauty, tranquility, and positive energy of the practice. I sincerely hope that you will take the time to understand what Falun Gong really is, to look at it with an open mind and heart, and to reject the politically motivated slander from the Chinese Communist Party. The world could use more Truthfulness, Compassion, and Forbearance.

Regaining the Happiness I Enjoyed As a Child

By a practitioner in China

My father died in a car accident when I was still a first-year middle school student. He left some property behind, and all the relatives from my father's side of the family plunged into a fight for it. My mother was traumatized by what happened. After the loss of my father, the inhumanity that the family members showed toward each other in fighting for the money, along with the neighbors' bad treatment of us, had a big effect on me. I became an eccentric person, did not trust people, and worshipped money. When I was in the third year of middle school, my mother remarried. My stepfather was a very honest and good-natured person, but I regarded this as cowardice. He did not worship money so much, and I considered that to be a sign of his incompetence. He did not demand too much from life, and I took that as a lack of ambition. I never called him "Dad." Though we lived under the same roof, our hearts were miles apart. My mother did not have any education. She was very reserved and also in very bad health. Since my childhood, we had difficulty communicating with each other. Out of vanity I thought that she would be of no help getting me to the top in society.

At school I worried that my classmates would look down upon me if they knew my family background and would bully me, so I never took the initiative to socialize with them. Even when I said something to them, I told lies. I lived my life with a mask on. I felt like I was a stranger in this world, and I could hardly believe anyone. At night I often cried under my quilt while I blamed everyone and complained about everything. In my head, I thought about how to end my own life many times, but I wasn't reconciled to such a thought because I still wanted revenge. I still wanted the family members from my father's side to fall on their knees to beg for my mercy, though I did not know how to achieve this. I was so disturbed by such thoughts that I was not at ease for even a single moment. How I wished I could return to my childhood, when I lived happily and was carefree every day.

At that time, my mom missed my dad very much and she was not able to get along well with my stepfather. My stepfather had a child from his previous marriage. The family members from my father's side continued to harass her, and all of these conflicts worsened my mother's health. Since modern medicine could not cure her diseases, my mom turned to practicing Falun Gong. Three months later she was rid of all of her illnesses.

I was so amazed by the miraculous effect of Falun Gong on curing illnesses. Out of curiosity I began to read the book *Zhuan Falun*. This book is a real treasure! It opened my heart—a heart that had been sealed and covered in dust. I came to the understanding that nothing that happened in this world was accidental, that there was a causal relationship behind everything. Whether you come across a good thing or a bad thing, as long as your mind is right and you follow the principles of "Truthfulness, Compassion, Forbearance," you will elevate your character.

I no longer complained, and I started to mingle with my family members. I remember that when I called my stepfather "Dad" for the first time, he was so excited that his eyes were shining with tears. Since then my home has been full of laughter and joy. I am able to communicate freely and sincerely with other people again. I treat everyone, including the family members from my father's side, with a true heart, and I no longer have the thought of committing suicide. I am filled with vitality and energy. At last I regained the happiness I had when I was a child.

My old classmates, whom I had not seen for a long time, marvel at the miracles Falun Dafa has created. I wrote down my experience with the hope that whoever reads this article will experience the same miracle through practicing Falun Gong themselves.

The Most Fortunate Beings in the Cosmos

By Francis Thurlow, U.K.

The age of 89 may seem a bit late to start a new commitment for the remainder of one's life. Two and a half years ago I received out of the blue a letter from an old friend telling me about Falun Gong, of which I had not previously heard. We had not been in contact for ten years, but we had practiced another spiritual path together, and I knew that he would not commit himself without very good reason. We met and talked and he gave me a copy of the main text of Falun Gong, *Zhuan Falun*.

I had an inner sense that I was being given a great opportunity after 30 years of frustrated spiritual search.

Like most people in the West, I had not had much contact with China, or with what has been a pretty remote cultural universe of Chinese Buddhism and Taoism. No doubt many of us have found that it is not easy to grasp some of the translated Chinese terminology. Taoist understanding of energy had hardly begun to penetrate the West before acupuncture entered the scene. These must have been familiar problems for others, and they confront us in seeking to spread the practice.

Once I started practicing, however, I felt encouraged. The

exercises have given me more energy. I need an hour's less sleep and expect to reduce this even further. I have always enjoyed good health, but the aftermath of three bouts of pneumonia over the years had left a constantly recurring cough, which has now disappeared. I'd had a tiresome skin ailment for three years, for which on advice I had arranged surgery. But I canceled the surgery, and the condition cleared up completely in a few weeks.

The West has had its own unacknowledged Great Cultural Revolution in the last 100 years when its belief system and values were almost entirely submerged in populist assumptions by the shallow metaphysics of a materialist science. Materialism, accompanied by a naive faith in technology as the solution to every problem, has swept over every continent at an accelerating pace, leaving in its wake the wreckage of traditional values, in spite of efforts by a minority of people to cling to them. But we have been given the answers to all the main problems in *Zhuan Falun*. Each time I read it, new depths of truth leap out.

We all know that Master Li has, by his saving presence and unceasing work, filled the moral void and, in the immense sweep of his vision, revealed a new rational understanding of the cosmos. Shock treatment may be inevitable as part of divine therapy for what we are doing to the world. But a healthier, less selfish and more cooperative global world community will emerge, showing in the human sphere that the essential qualities of all life, as of the Great Universe, are Truthfulness, Compassion and Forbearance.

I have myself witnessed first hand the global degeneration, seeing in Asia, Africa and the Americas, as well as in Europe, the erosion of traditional values.

I entered Diplomatic Service on leaving Cambridge, spending 40 years divided equally between the Foreign and Commonwealth Office at home and service abroad, specializing in Commonwealth relations, a constantly evolving process as the British Empire was transformed into 50 independent countries. A child in the first World War, after the second I attended Peace Conferences and the early meetings of the United Nations, and went on to strenuous and responsible work in India, Canada, Ghana, New Zealand and Australia, Nigeria and the Bahamas. On retirement I spent 15 years in the House of Lords.

I was brought up by parents who sought to apply in their lives the teaching of Jesus on truth, love and humility. And facing hardship and overcoming attachments had been at the core of my previous spiritual path, which I tried to work on after retirement for ten years, with some years devoted to yoga. So I was helped by my background to grasp the special character of the opportunity when it came.

Writing this article has itself helped me to face up to my own daunting spectrum of failings. There is, of course, no end to what should be done in working on attachments; mental ones are more difficult than physical. As a human being I am largely unaware of them. I am a moral coward, not wanting to be laughed at, even though it can obviously do no harm. How absurd! I am stuck in my life-style and used to a soft life. It is tempting in old age to opt out of activity, making increasing limitations an excuse and carrying on with former interests. All your priorities must eventually change when you undertake the practice.

Even at so late a stage I know that I have found my way at last with a new horizon, a fresh understanding and, thanks to the exercises, more energy. But that misses the point. We have been given an inconceivable privilege, and I certainly regard myself as one of the luckiest men of my generation.

We have been given an inconceivable gift and we face the challenge to be worthy of it and to do more to give others the same opportunity.

Finding Meaning in My Life

By Zhen Lijuan, China

Veteran practitioners have already experienced what I am about to discuss. The purpose of writing this article is to sincerely encourage those who have just started this cultivation practice, as well as those who have not yet begun. I hope you can all share my joy in finding new meaning in life, in getting rid of illnesses, and in elevating one's character from practicing Falun Dafa.

In ancient and modern times, the most difficult thing in a family for a young woman is to get along with her mother-in-law. I do not mean to make critical comments about other people, but the real cause of all the hardship in my family was that we were all against Truthfulness, Compassion, Forbearance. In short, before I began to practice, my family was already on the brink of breaking apart. My husband and I were on the verge of divorce. In order to release the pain in my heart, I used to read some spiritual books, but they didn't give me much help. At that time I felt that I had no way out. My daughter and I had illnesses. My family fought all the time and were cold to one another. I was suffering from both within and without.

I felt hopeless, and didn't know how I should spend the rest of my life. For the past ten years, our rancor had piled up mountain-high. There are sayings like "Take one step back, the ocean is broader and the sky is clearer;" "Forgiving others is one's joy;" and "No excuse for getting ill from being angry." I understood these sayings theoretically, and I tried to smile at my sadness. But my heart didn't feel that way. My body and mind were suffering all the time.

On October 9, 1998, I began practicing Falun Dafa. When a practitioner handed *Zhuan Falun* to me, she told me that this book was very precious. I didn't realize that I had started a new life as I opened this book. Although I love reading books, I had never found a book like *Zhuan Falun* that could inspire me so much. The words in this book are of great compassion and awe-inspiring righteousness. I couldn't wait to read through the whole book right away. My point of view about life was changed greatly, though I still had many questions in my mind. What really amazed me was that I could forgive my husband and his mother, unbelievably, from my heart. I discovered the things that I had done wrong, that had caused me such unforgettable pain and had haunted me for such a long time. I was contrite about hurting their feelings. The most difficult step was to admit my own wrongdoing and not complain about others; even bow to the person that hurt me. Ten years of hatred was released in one day. Only *Zhuan Falun* could have such a power!

A few days after I read the book, my husband suddenly got sick. He was sent to the emergency room. I stayed with him the whole time and took care of him with a sincere heart. I remembered one time when I had arthritis and wanted to see a doctor, he accused me of pretending sickness just to spend money. Now when he was sick, I took time off from work to take care of him. I could finally return his hatred with my virtue. After this adversity, my family gained good fortune and has been reunited. I know that my husband's illness was not accidental. It came on so fiercely, yet disappeared all of a sudden. And its outcome was that it has brought us from the edge of divorce to reunion.

After that, I played a tape from Master Li's nine-day lecture series for my family, and in this way, they came to understand about improving character. They also learned that Dafa practitioners are good people who are guided by "Truthfulness, Compassion, Forbearance." Other family members have also benefited, even though they don't practice. For example, my mother-in-law used to be very devout in worshipping her god, while she cursed people behind their backs. Now she is careful about what she says. Furthermore, she used to not cook for my family. She probably thought that she wouldn't gain benefits from helping her daughter-in-law. We were constantly at odds with each other and helping each other was the last thing on our minds. Now, my mother-in-law prepares the meals every day. When I come home from work, everything is finished. Falun Dafa can help people to regain their kind nature.

After several months of practicing cultivation, I truly realized the truth that mind and matter are one thing. At that moment I woke up: birth, old age, illnesses, and death are facts of life in this world. The most terrible thing is a person who cannot distinguish between righteousness and evil. In the past, I always judged people based on my opinion of what they said and did. Now, when thinking about something or someone, I make sure that my mind follows the characteristic of the universe—Truthfulness, Compassion, Forbearance.

Falun Dafa Lifted Me Up And Made Me a Better Person

By Wang Tianxing, Singapore

In June 1998, a new colleague of mine gave me a copy of the "Falun Dafa Lecture in Sydney". It seemed like it was very easy for me to begin practicing Falun Dafa. That August, I met Master Li at the Singapore Experience Sharing Conference. Now looking back, I realize that I am indeed a very fortunate person.

As soon as I began to practice Falun Dafa, I loved to read the Falun Dafa books. Since then I have been constantly reading the books, which subsequently has had a positive effect on my ability to steadfastly cultivate in Dafa.

In November 1998, I attended a 9-day video lecture by Master Li and I started to practice the five sets of exercises. In the beginning, I realized that my enlightenment capacity was not very good. Although I loved to read Falun Dafa books, I could hardly remember anything afterwards, let alone understand some of the Fa and why we needed to study the Fa. Later, I went to a new practice site. With the help of other practitioners, I continued to study the Fa. I gradually began to understand the Fa and I came to a clearer understanding of what cultivation is all about. I then realized that *Zhuan Falun* is a book that genuinely guides people to practice cultivation.

Here I truly hope that those people who misunderstand or who don't know what Falun Dafa is could read *Zhuan Falun*, thus giving themselves a chance to know what it contains. What exactly is written in this book? What is Falun Dafa? Don't just follow the hearsay. One must understand the purpose and the meaning of life and one should be responsible for one's own life. I truly hope that everyone can come to personally experience Falun Dafa. Now, I shall relate some changes that I have experienced during my three years of cultivation.

I have been transformed from a sick person to a healthy man. Before I practiced Falun Gong, I would need to go to bed before 10 p.m. every night and when I woke up, my body would ache all over. My wife and son liked to go window-shopping during the weekend. This was an agonizing weekend duty for me. They were enthusiastically walking around while I kept looking for a chair to sit down and if possible to lie down and have some rest. Now, I don't feel tired all day long and I feel very energetic.

My mental health also changed tremendously. Before I practiced Falun Gong, I just didn't know how to smile and I hadn't smiled for many years. Happiness was a strange word to me. Now I've changed into a happy man, and I smile to greet people at anytime and I can face life's pressures and challenges optimistically.

I used to be an intolerant man. Frequently, I would flare up over family trifles and petty matters. Now, I can remain calm in any conflict, reflect on the matter, and self-reflect for any mistake I might have made in the conflict. I have

149

become a broad-minded man and now have a tolerant heart.

I used to be very mean, but now I take personal gain lightly and I have realized that many problems and conflicts were actually caused by my various attachments.

After I attended the experience-sharing conference in Taiwan in December 2000, I gradually developed a deeper understanding. At times, a word or sentence from a fellow practitioner could have a critical and intriguing effect on my advancement. Greater effects could be achieved if the word was incisive and could penetrate my heart. As long as one is able to always treat oneself as a practitioner and look inward, one will be able to quickly recognize one's attachments.

Master Li has repeatedly stressed the need to study the Fa. Some fellow practitioners have upgraded their character very quickly through studying the Fa. They took their own initiative in doing it, didn't rely on others, didn't wait for others and they put their hearts and minds into Dafa. I think this can be attributed to their constant study of the Fa and to their righteous understanding.

In the preface to *Zhuan Falun*, Master Li says, "'The Buddha Fa is most profound; among all the theories in the world, it is the most intricate and extraordinary science. In order to explore this domain, humankind must fundamentally change its conventional thinking. Otherwise, the truth of the universe will forever remain a mystery to humankind, and everyday people will forever crawl within the boundary delimited by their own ignorance."

This and other teachings from Master Li have opened up a whole new world for me, and made me into a different, better person.

Learning to Say, *"This Was My Fault"*

By a practitioner in China

One afternoon, while my four-year-old son was stepping on a chair to get a pear from the table, he fell down and overturned a half plate of rice I had put on the table. As he lay there on the floor, his body covered with rice, my first reaction was that I needed to calm down. My son was apparently fine, so I pulled him up, and then cleaned the carpet where he fell. I found that I was not angry and also aware that this incident was my fault, as I did not clean up the table immediately after finishing lunch.

Previously, when my children spilled or dropped anything, I instinctively thought that it was their fault and scolded them. Later I felt this behavior was not benevolent, and I needed to pay attention and improve in this area. I finally changed this bad habit and looked at myself when something went wrong. I sincerely admitted to my son that this was my fault and reminded him that he should be careful in the future. He nodded his head. At this moment, I felt a peaceful atmosphere spread in the air. Persistently cultivating myself and changing my wrong notions, I finally realized that I could treat other people with benevolence and forgiveness from my heart. This made me feel so good inside. I felt in my heart, how fortunate I am to know these eternal truths and to have the opportunity to cultivate myself under the boundless mercy of Master Li. I felt happy, fortunate, and at peace after improving myself.

One day after this incident, my son overturned half a bowl of soup. I said immediately, without any hesitation, "It's all right. Are you OK?" Then I cleaned up the soup with a paper towel. I gently said to my son, "You need to be careful next time." This warmed the heart of everyone in my family. Since this incident, my son has seldom spilled anything.

One day, my husband couldn't find the nail clippers. He was in a bad mood and accused me of misplacing them somewhere. He was so infuriated that before he left the house to go out and play with the kids, he told me, "Find the nail clippers before I return!" At that moment, the atmosphere was full of tension. Then my son said to my husband, "If when we come back, Mom still has not found the nail clippers, you just say it's all right!" My son learned forgiveness. So, in the end, the result was really, "It's all right!"

In my mind I thought, "My reward is not only in my own cultivation, but also the opportunity I've had to influence my son." Just as Master Li said, "The Buddha light illuminates everywhere, Propriety and justice rectify and harmonize everything."

Our Class Is Now Well Behaved

By a young practitioner in Taiwan

I am a sixth-grade student attending elementary school. Shortly after school began this semester, my teacher asked us to read a book called *Zhuan Falun*. She also taught the students in my class how to do the Falun Gong exercises.

I have found that reading this book has been very good for me. Before I read *Zhuan Falun*, I would easily lose my temper, but now I have learned to control it better. Sometimes I would also fight with my younger brother, but now I never fight with him, as my temperament has also improved. Before the students started to practice Falun Gong, we were very noisy and would fight with each other during our break time. Since we started to practice Falun Gong, we behave very well.

Before, when the boys in my class decided they disliked a certain girl, I followed them and stopped talking to her. After reading *Zhuan Falun*, I went to her and apologized, which made her very happy. When the boys say bad words to her, she wants to retaliate and return the abuse, but I convince her not to do so. Through this, we've become good friends.

A while ago, I read *Zhuan Falun* twice, but I still didn't

understand what genuine cultivation practice was. Now, I have finally realized that the principles stated in *Zhuan Falun* need to be applied in our daily lives.

I will spend my summer holiday time diligently reading *Zhuan Falun* and practicing the exercises. I will take care of my younger brother and I will never fight with him. I will never say bad words to other students and moreover I will change my bullying character and get along with my classmates.

Certainly, I must thank the author of *Zhuan Falun*, our great, merciful Master.

Falun Dafa Is Deeply Rooted In My Heart

By Yu Lukun, Rochester, New York, U.S.A.

The first time I heard about Falun Gong was back in May 1994, when I went back to China to visit my family. I quickly flipped through *Zhuan Falun* and found it too deep to understand. After we returned to the States, my husband couldn't stop talking about how good Falun Gong is. I kept wondering how he, with a doctoral and a master's degree in science, could be so into qigong. The first time we received the audiotapes of Master Li's Nine-Day Lecture in Jinan, my husband and I anxiously finished the tapes within two days. I was saying to myself, "So, that was the truth of life! It sounded reasonable, but is it real?" How could I give up the idea of seeking material interests as the purpose of life? It was too difficult for me.

Then in October 1995, my mother died of cancer. I was in deep shock and thought a lot. I couldn't understand why she would leave this world at the age when she could enjoy her life after decades of hard work. Under the influence of my husband, I tried to read the book several times but never finished it due to the strong attachments I had and other forms of interference.

In March 1997, I was fortunate enough to attend

the Falun Dafa Conference in New York City and listen to Master Li's lecture. At that time I still had not finished reading *Zhuan Falun* and was full of all kinds of attachments. I had only vague ideas of what Master Li was saying, but I could feel an unspeakable force shaking very hard in the bottom of my heart. After the conference, my husband asked me if I would become a true cultivator. I said yes. Then, the very next day, my watch and diamond ring disappeared when I was staying at my friend's house. They were nowhere to be found.

I also faced tribulations and conflicts with my mother-in-law. I have never been able to get along with my mother-in-law since I married my husband. I am a strong-minded person. I'm always concerned about how other people think of me and fear their criticizing or taking advantage of me. My mother-in-law is a straight-forward person with a sharp tongue, and she favors her son. In her eyes, I can never do right while he is never wrong. When I had my first child in 1995, she came to help and stayed with us. There were conflicts, one after the other. I was very stressed out and upset to the point that I couldn't stand her any more. I complained to my husband constantly. He turned around and tried to comfort me by showing me what Master Li said in *Zhuan Falun*, but I just couldn't get over the fact that I had to abide by Dafa, enduring and forgiving. After attending the conference in 1997, I realized that I couldn't keep avoiding the obstacles. I made up my mind and prepared myself for anything to come. Sure enough, the next day when we were doing housework together, my mother-in-law started complaining about me sarcastically. Since I was prepared, I was able to keep my composure the whole time.

After that I thought I did pretty well. During that period, I stayed home raising my child and did not go out much. Life was quiet and simple, but my mind did not remain quiet or tranquil. The unfairness and negative comments from my mother-in-law kept popping up in my mind. I did not pay much attention to it at first, but gradually I started to get into fights with her in my mind. Even though I had started practicing the exercises, I did not spend much time reading Master Li's books. I was the same person. Nothing had changed deep in my heart. I became resentful. I even felt that I was rather stupid not to protect my own interests when I was tested. I should reason with her and decide who is right and wrong. Little by little I went back to being an ordinary person.

Although I had stopped studying the teachings and exercising, I still liked to watch videotapes of Master Li's lectures at various locations and read other practitioners' experience-sharing articles. Feeling depressed, though, I was not willing to let go of my attachment to fame, interests and sentimentality. Dafa sounded great but it was impossible for me to live up to.

The problem dragged on until March 1998, when my husband went to the New York conference and brought back Master Li's lecture tapes. Once again I picked up Zhuan Falun. I told myself this time that I should not put down the book until I finished it. Finally, four years after I first heard about Falun Gong, I finished Zhuan Falun, and once more I became determined to be a true cultivator.

Immediately following came a test regarding sentimentality between husband and wife. I was very sentimental and self-pitying, valuing very much the affection between husband and wife. My heart would twist and turn whenever my husband did not treat me right or pay attention to me. It was impossible for me to take this sentimentality lightly, let alone give it up. This attachment had been a big barrier preventing me from being a true cultivator. During that time, for whatever reason, I did not get to spend much time with my husband, and I felt neglected. It seemed as if it were all his fault. I tried to talk to him a few times, but my effort was in vain. I was confused. Once when I was reading, I came across Master Li's words: "Whenever there is interference of one kind or another in qigong practice, you should look for reasons within yourself and determine what you still have not let go." (*Zhuan Falun*) Later in a discussion with another practitioner on the issue, she quoted Master Li as saying we should look inward whenever there is a conflict. I realized that the real cause of the issue still was inside of me, no matter how it looked to be his fault superficially. My emotions weighed too heavily on me. I was accusing my husband, feeling my own interests were hurt. I was covering myself using Master Li's words and going against the true nature of the universe. Having realized the truth, I still found it too hard to let go of the attachment. Feeling the pain of not being able to let go of the attachment, I kept reading the books to help resist the evil thoughts and gradually I found the attachment becoming more and more trivial. Gradually my relationship with my husband became harmonious. I have never felt so relieved in my life.

I am a full-time working mother with a two-year-old and a four-year-old. Every day I get up at the crack of dawn and by the time I go to bed, it is usually ten or eleven o'clock. I squeeze in time to read and exercise when the kids are playing after dinner. I used to play with my kids inattentively and try to hide myself away from them whenever I could. The less I wanted them to find me, the more they would find me. Sometimes I wished I could have a cultivation environment like practitioners with no children. With such a wrong mentality, I had little patience with the kids. Sometimes I was angry with them. Very soon, I was asking myself what had happened and where was my compassion? Why couldn't I always put others before myself? Isn't the most difficult environment the best opportunity for improvement for a practitioner? So I started watching Master Li's nine-day lecture videos with them and I read *Zhuan Falun* to them. Since I have calmed myself, the children have changed as well. My four-year-old insists on having me read the book when he goes to bed. The little one doesn't allow me to turn the light off until she falls asleep, so I can read while sitting by her bed.

Even though I made up my mind to be a cultivator again in 1998, I still failed to improve the bumpy relationship with my mother-in-law. I had chosen to stay away from her to minimize unnecessary contact. At the beginning of this year, my parents-in-law decided to visit us again in the U.S. I was quite nervous at the time and did not wish them to come. I told my husband, "We are absolutely able to take care of our kids by ourselves. All you want is to lie back, since your parents will help you. What's wrong with us enduring a bit more hardship?" I knew that I was wrong, but still used Dafa as an excuse to cover myself up. Believe it or not, my parents-in-law decided not to apply for visas after all. The trip was postponed. I thought to myself that I had lucked out

I attended the New York Falun Dafa conference in March of 1999. I was deeply moved by other practitioners' cultivation experiences, and I was also able to find where I lagged behind. The day after I came back home, my parents-in-law phoned and said that they were going to apply for visas. Several days later, we learned that they would visit that May. At this time, I began to calm down and realized that my attachment could not be gotten rid of without a difficult environment. My "fear" of facing my mother-in-law was in itself an attachment that I must let go of.

On the day of my in-laws' arrival, I volunteered to pick them up at the airport. For the following days, I encountered many opportunities to improve my character. Sometimes I was able to overcome the obstacle and sometimes not. There were occasions when I seemed to conduct myself according to Dafa, but it was not from the bottom of my heart. When that happened, the same obstacle would occur again. In every conflict, if my attachment surfaced, the atmosphere would change negatively too. After arriving, my parents-in-law planted many kinds of vegetables in the back yard and spent a lot of time and effort gardening. One day after I came back from work, my mother-in-law told me that some of the newly grown plants were cut evenly, as if by a pair of scissors. She questioned me and made oblique accusations. I immediately sensed that she suspected me. I felt unfairly treated and upset. Very soon I calmed down and realized that what had just happened was not accidental. I did not have the right mindset when I was answering her questions and was only concerned about being wrongly blamed, and

I did not put myself in her shoes. Once I calmed down, I started to help her find out what had happened to the plants. Later I put a garden fence around the vegetables. A few days later, my mother-in-law told me that she had discovered that it was a squirrel that had eaten the plants.

During one of the conversations with my husband, I said that my mother-in-law seemed to have changed this time. He responded, "I don't think she has changed. She still speaks the same way and treats you the same way. It is you who has changed." Before going back to China, my father-in-law said to me, "You have become mature since you started practicing Falun Gong. Your mother-in-law has not made any negative comments about you in front of me yet." My mother-in-law also said to me, "How can you be so energetic after a long busy day?"

Ever since July 1999, Dafa has encountered unprecedented tribulations. Like many other practitioners, I went to Washington D.C. While there, I had many opportunities to work with other practitioners to promote Dafa. I saw how other practitioners were always trying to understand everything based upon the principles of Dafa. Whatever they did or said, it always had to be with compassionate hearts and a calm and peaceful manner. By contrast, I found myself nervous, unsettled, and easily excited, but I realized that it was indeed a good cultivation environment and I found myself understanding quite a bit.

Initially I thought I would be in D.C. for only a day. After I arrived, I felt that I should stay longer. Then I was wondering how to ask my boss for time off. I work for a small company and I have responsibilities that are difficult for others to cover. There was a project pushing a deadline.

However, I had only one thought in my mind: I had to stay even at the cost of my job. I phoned my boss and tried my best to explain to him the situation and my willingness to make up with overtime as soon as I got back. My boss was not very happy and hinted that I might lose my job. After the conversation, I was worried most of the day. Letting go of the attachment of personal interest is always easier said than done. After repeated mental struggles, I uncovered my attachments of fear, fame and personal gain. After coming back from D.C., I had a frank conversation with my boss. I also completed my project on time. Two weeks later, my boss gave me a raise.

Looking back at my cultivation path, I nearly passed by Dafa. Master Li's benevolence has been giving me opportunities all along. He handed me this great law of the universe and helped purify my body. Master Li takes every single opportunity to help me abandon all my attachments to become a true practitioner. He helped me discover the truth of life. I know I still have a lot of attachments to get rid of and have a long way to go in my cultivation. However, Dafa is deeply rooted in my heart. Nothing and nobody can shake my determination and resolve to be a true cultivator!

Separating the Chaff from the Pure Essence

By Arleen Freeman, San Diego, California, U.S.A.

I have been a Falun Gong practitioner for a little over one year. I feel as if I have been going through a threshing process. So many events have happened to separate the chaff from the pure essence of who I am.

I first attended a practice site in November of 1999. At first I did not understand very much, but I kept reading and kept cultivating and some remarkable things have happened to me.

I have changed so much. Before Falun Gong I suffered from Post Traumatic Stress Disorder (PTSD) because I had been the victim of a very violent crime. I had difficulty sleeping. I thought I needed alcohol to fall asleep at night. Even though the man who committed this crime was tried and put in jail for the rest of his life, I lived in constant fear of being attacked. I never wanted to go home and when I did go home, I locked myself in my bedroom.

Within two months I stopped therapy, and eventually all my symptoms disappeared. I am calm and serene. My energy level has increased dramatically. I am highly focused on my work and I am very successful.

I am a real estate agent and property manager. I hired a

roofer recommended by a friend of mine to install a new roof over a garage. I gave the roofer a deposit of half down and he started removing the old roof the next day. The only problem was that he removed the next-door neighbor's roof, not the one I had hired him to do.

Needless to say the people storing things in the neighbor's garage were very angry. They kept yelling at the roofer to stop and he kept telling them that they were not the owner and he did not work for them. Many of their things were damaged because old roofing material kept falling onto their things during the removal process. Finally someone called me and I told the roofer it was the wrong roof. He quit, leaving no covering at all on the neighbor's garage. The neighbor was very angry with me and insisted I fix the roof. Since the man I hired did not have a contractor's license, he could refuse me, knowing there was nothing I could do. Luckily it did not rain. This went on for a week.

Ultimately, although I was a new practitioner, I knew this was my responsibility. I finally made the decision that I would hire another roofer, this time one with a contractor's license, and pay the entire cost myself. I knew there was no other choice. The very day I hired another contractor, the original roofer finished the job. I repeatedly told the people whose things were damaged that I would be responsible for the repairs, but to this day they have never asked me for anything.

I don't think there could be a more vivid way to teach me about giving up my attachment to saving money or about being responsible.

This happened after I had only been a practitioner for a

few months. Another incident happened just recently and has had a much deeper effect.

I had a friend, a fellow practitioner, with whom I discussed many things. We made many observations about other people, often criticizing them. All of this was extremely interesting and enlightening until one day my friend criticized me. I thought his criticism was extremely unfair. I know that in a conflict we must look inside ourselves. I realized the extent to which I had criticized others. I blamed others. I found fault with others. Whether I said anything to them or not, I judged them. It just did not feel right when I was the one being judged.

Then I understood. I needed to be paid back for all those times I had judged others, criticized others, and hurt others because my motives were never pure. I realized that I needed to be hurt in order to pay back the hurt I had caused others. I needed to feel pain in order to pay back the pain I had caused others. I became very withdrawn and started to feel actual physical pain in my left arm. This pain seemed very, very fitting. It seemed to be getting worse. It got to the point where I could not lift my arm to do the second exercise because it hurt too much.

Then I read what Master Li said about criticism in "Teaching the Fa at the Conference in Singapore:"

"I often say that if a person is free of any personal notions, isn't motivated by self-interest, and is truly looking to benefit others, then when he points out another person's shortcoming or tells the other person what's right, that person will be moved to tears."

At the following weekend's practice, I could lift my arm and the pain was almost gone. I knew that the unjust criticism from my friend was a message that I could use to purify myself so that I could separate the chaff from the pure essence of who I am.

How I Resolved a Long-Term Conflict with My Husband

By Zhao Meihua, China

Before I started practicing Falun Dafa, both my husband and I had short tempers and would never yield to each other. We spent most of our time fighting. Then my husband was sentenced to prison and his family also had several accidents. I asked my mother-in-law to live with me and led her to practice Dafa. Three years later my husband was released. Although he had no income he spent money freely while I tried to be thrifty. I tried to tolerate him, but he still picked on me. Once, over a minor issue, he pointed his finger at my nose and insulted me in the presence of my mother-in-law and my friends. I was miserable and often cried.

Since I practice Dafa, I understood the principles and realized that I needed to practice forbearance. When I encountered conflicts, I always tried to improve my character, but because I did not look within and find my attachments, the conflicts still continued. I still could not always control my temper. This went on for a long time.

It was after carefully reading the *Nine Commentaries on the Communist Party* four times that I truly found my attachment : the heart of fighting. It has been deeply rooted in me for many years. Sometimes it comes out without my even knowing it.

When I looked within, I found that when I talked to my husband, I always had an unyielding attitude and challenging tone of voice. I had not had a heart-to-heart conversation with him since he had returned from prison. Although I tolerated him superficially, I looked down on him in my heart. I thought, "You are dependent on my salary, but now you want to control me. If I were not a practitioner, I would have divorced you."

With this kind of thinking I could not really care for him or think well of him. Usually he did the grocery shopping and bought the vegetables, but when he got home, I was always unhappy with what he had bought. Understandably, this agitated him. One time he spent nearly 100 *yuan* to buy a bouquet for my birthday. I not only did not thank him, but I also complained that he had spent too much money. He was initially very happy but became depressed after that.

In retrospect, all of this was my fault. I had always wanted to be strong. Before cultivation, I had the nickname "Superwoman" and would never yield to others. After beginning my cultivation, although I could tolerate fellow practitioners and friends, I could not do it at home. My behavior was far from the standard of a practitioner. How could I achieve "Truthfulness, Compassion, Forbearance?" My cultivation state varied all the time.

A fellow practitioner said that there are no shortcuts in cultivation and only by studying the Fa well can we look within, change ourselves, and improve. If we are not compassionate with our family members who have shortcomings, it is as if we are not cultivating. His words inspired me.

Once I found my attachment, I changed my attitude. Now I see my husband's strong points and my own shortcomings. I care for him and am more considerate. Because of my change of heart, my husband has changed his attitude toward me and toward Falun Dafa. Initially he claimed that he would send me to the Public Security Bureau. Now he has come to understand and support Dafa. He often helps me to buy tapes, repair the tape recorder, and maintain the Dafa books. So that I could study the Fa at night, he bought several desk lamps and clamped one to the bed. On "World Falun Dafa Day," he ordered a cake with three white lotus flowers on top because his mother, myself, and our granddaughter are all practitioners.

While I was writing this article, I asked my husband to buy some paper. He forgot and only remembered it once he got home. He then went back out to get it. The change in his attitude has made the whole family happy and has positively influenced our daughter. She bought me a cell phone for Dafa work. They all withdrew from the Chinese Communist Party, too.

My cultivation environment is becoming better and better, and I have come to a deeper understanding of Master Li's teachings.

When I Was Seeking Revenge, I Found Zhuan Falun Instead

By a practitioner in China

Before learning Falun Gong, I had a really bad temper. I was very short fused, and often made a big deal out of trivial issues. I picked on my wife. I liked to break things when I had a tantrum, and I felt quite exhilarated afterwards. My mental breakdowns often scared my kids, and agonized my wife to the point of crying. My family was on the brink of breaking up. Away from home, I was the one who had to have the last word. I was crazy about money, and would fight to the last penny. I wouldn't mind going to jail for the right amount of money. I was extremely jealous. Due to my own bad temperament, I suffered poor health with numerous illnesses, such as migraine headaches, high blood pressure, bronchitis, and a slipped disk in my lower back that pressed against the nerves of my legs. I could not even take care of myself if it flared up. I couldn't even turn over in bed. I was suffering beyond words.

One incident finally caused me to give up all hope. Some hoodlums and deputies in the County Police Department conspired to swindle 50,000 *yuan* out of me in a business deal. They even threw me in the County Detention Center for 15 days. Even the jail guard was angry about this conspiracy, and urged me to file a lawsuit against the police after I got out. I traveled far to file my lawsuit papers to the Director of Public Safety. Yet, the director told me, "Even if they are convicted, you won't get your money back." I had no place to file my complaint even though I was in the right. I had no place to appeal, even when I had been wrongly accused. From this point on, the people that I hated most were the police. It has been said, "Ten years is not a long wait for a person seeking revenge." I thought about buying a gun. I would get revenge by killing these parasites fattened by the blood and sweat of the people. I would get rid of these hoodlums for the people. That was the one and only thought then on my mind.

While I was looking for a gun all over the place, I was fortunate to instead come upon Master Li's book, *Zhuan Falun*. I read the book from cover to cover in one pass. I realized why we live as humans, and how to live as a human. Today, mankind's ideologies are built upon self-interest. Everyone has sinned while lost in this labyrinth. If you mistreat me, I will treat you even worse. People will kill over trivial issues. I finally understood the principle of "rewards and consequences will await both good and bad deeds," and, "One will pay back for one's own bad deeds." Master Li said, "Many people just live to prove their point or save face and will hang themselves when they cannot deal with things anymore." (*Zhuan Falun*) Was it worthwhile? I was like a balloon with all its air let out. My criminal intention to kill for revenge was totally uprooted and dispersed. It was Master Li who saved me from a potential catastrophe in my life. The outcome would have been unthinkable.

Since I have practiced Falun Dafa, my explosive temper has disappeared, together with my jealousy. My lower back pain and headaches are all miraculously gone, just like my other illnesses. My body is in good health. My family life is much more harmonious and perfectly satisfactory. Gone are the sounds of arguments and squabbles. My cultivation still has a long way to go. When others hurt my feelings, I cannot quite be at ease with them. Sometimes I will still be mad inside myself. Master Li has said that forbearance is the key to improving one's character, and that to endure with hatred, grievances or tears is the forbearance of an ordinary person who is attached to his misgivings. To bear without any hatred or grievance at all is the forbearance of a practitioner. I can do much more to improve on my forbearance, as I am far short of the level of Master Li's requirement. But at least I can control myself and not hurt others, and not fight with others.

I can see the vast difference in myself before and after cultivation practice. It is Falun Dafa that transformed me, and that allowed me to see the hope and glory. Master Li has taught us how to build an unselfish, considerate, righteous attitude through cultivation. One should return to one's original, true self.

This is why all over the country, Falun Dafa practitioners are adopting various means to clarify the truth about the persecution. They are willing to face the tremendous pressure, risking their lives and careers to step forward. Many of them have been imprisoned without reason, and many have suffered atrocious tortures. They are facing and braving everything while following the principles of "Truthfulness, Compassion, and Forbearance."

The Best Decision I Ever Made: Reflecting On My First Year as a Falun Dafa Practitioner

By a practitioner in China

As I grew older and experienced many ups-and-downs in my life, I felt sad and sorry that I was born into a world where people fight when their self-interests are infringed upon in the slightest way. "Why has mankind fallen so low and become so corrupt?" I asked in despair. "Where can I find a piece of pure land?" From elementary school to college, I often had the desire to explore the mysteries of life.

In 1998, I graduated from a university and started my career. I never stopped my search for the meaning of life. I tried to find answers in books of all kinds: philosophy, Buddhism, history, etc. I would pick up a book full of hope, but end up putting it down in disappointment.

Finally, I stopped looking for answers. I put my heart into poetry, literature, music, and having fun with friends. Although I was busy, I had a sense of being lost and felt sorrow deep in my heart, so much so that I hid from others at times.

Seemingly by a chance, something happened that changed my life at the time of the 2002 Chinese New Year. Right before the Chinese New Year festivities began, I received several emails about Falun Gong. They claimed that the persecution of Falun Gong was "the greatest injustice in history," and that "China Central Television was framing Falun Gong." Because the information in the emails was so different from the official propaganda, I thought it was not very believable.

I went back to my hometown during the Chinese New Year. While chatting with my father, who is a policeman, I learned that Falun Gong practitioners are indeed not like the people described in the Chinese media. On the contrary, they really are good people, surprisingly good people. I was very surprised and confused at the same time. "If they are such good people," I wondered, "then why is the government spreading such a big lie and making so much effort against them?"

After the Chinese New Year, I went back to work in City A. Driven by my curiosity, I tried to use the Internet to get more information about Falun Gong. I wanted to visit the Minghui/Clearwisdom website and see what Falun Gong was all about. When I couldn't break through the Internet blockade, I visited a colleague's mother when I heard that she practiced Falun Gong.

This lady kindly told me about Falun Gong and described her family situation. She told me about the changes she had experienced since she started practicing in 1996. She told me that her whole family lived in harmony until 1999, when Falun Gong began to be slandered and persecuted by Jiang Zemin and the Chinese Communist Party. Hearing her story was like waking up from a dream. I was shocked by what had happened in the land of China.

When I got back home I watched the video CD she had given me. The video showed an elderly farmer who had walked to Tiananmen Square from Shanxi province just to tell people that Falun Dafa is good. On his journey, he lived and camped in the open, and had worn out nine pairs of shoes. The video showed how the government mischaracterized the appeal that took place on April 25, 1999, yet the picture showed the facts: about ten thousand Falun Gong practitioners had peacefully appealed to the government. This is a government that has a reputation for brutality. Yet so many people, knowing they could face death, were willing to disregard their own lives and appeal on behalf of Falun Gong. They looked so calm, so peaceful, and so unperturbed.

Here was a group of ordinary citizens who were willing to sacrifice so much: not for fame, not for self-interest, but only to clarify the truth to everyone. I was deeply moved by their extraordinary heroism. When I saw that people kept holding up their banners on Tiananmen Square with the words, "Truthfulness-Compassion-Forbearance," even when the police were beating them, I could not stop my tears. With extraordinary actions, these people demonstrated unbelievable selflessness and great virtue! They were clearly using their lives to protect kindness, to defend justice, and to call out to others' consciences. In an instant, the banners they held above their heads with the three words, "Truthfulness-Compassion-Forbearance," made me understand everything they were doing. At that moment, I made the best decision in my life, a decision I will never regret: "I want to be one of them."

On that day, March 3, 2002, I declared to my friends, "I want to be a Falun Gong practitioner." Seeing their astonished looks, I earnestly explained to them, "Falun Gong practitioners have been wrongly accused. They are good people, and they are being persecuted! I am going to tell everyone I know about the truth of the persecution!" In the atmosphere of violence and intimidation in China, and out of concern for my safety, my friends immediately called my father and informed him of this shocking news. My father rushed to see me the very next day.

My father lectured me for a long time, and I also heard my mother crying over the phone. They were deeply hurt by my "impulsive" decision. My father knew that Falun Gong is good. In his eyes, however, I was like a moth flying into a flame; my mother didn't understand the truth, and she believed that a person should just go with the flow in all situations. They pressured me to give up my choice. My father even threatened to sever our father-son relationship. Because I chose to cultivate in Falun Gong, my family might become divided, I might lose my job, and I might be put in jail and persecuted at any moment. All of a sudden, I faced a pressure I had never experienced before. At that moment, I began to experience firsthand the unimaginable difficulties behind every step and every decision made by those Falun Gong practitioners. The scene from Tiananmen Square where the banners were recurrently held up high by the practitioners came to my mind. Deep inside my soul a voice told me, "For justice, for compassion, I will never give in!" Finally, I told my father, "Dad, I do not regret my decision. Even if I am going to be put in jail and beaten to death, I will not regret it." Knowing he could not change my mind, my father left feeling disappointed and worried three days later.

I started to study Master Li's books, from *Essentials for Further Advancement* and *Guiding the Voyage*, to *Zhuan Falun*. Although my understanding was not deep, my soul was deeply touched over and over again. I was moved and convinced by the profound principles of the Fa. My wish to cultivate became firmer and firmer. All my doubts about human society and life disappeared. I no longer felt self-pity from living in a world full of evil and deceit. I no longer felt lost because I lacked purpose and direction in life. I no longer felt sad for all those sentient beings who could not escape the misery of having feelings such as resentment and hatred. On the contrary, I felt fortunate to be living in the time when Falun Dafa is spreading around the world. I felt very proud of choosing the path of cultivation, because this is the path along which I can return to my true self. I felt joyful and encouraged for the infinite grace and compassion that have come to the human world.

I started to learn the exercises, and went from doing the single leg crossing position to doing the double leg crossing position. I endured fatigue during the standing meditation, and the discomfort of the sitting meditation. I became more convinced that Falun Dafa is true to its name and reputation. My confidence in practicing grew, as well.

Looking back over the past year, I have changed from being hostile towards Dafa to becoming a Dafa practitioner. I am grateful to the unknown practitioner who sent me the email, my father, and my colleague's mother. If it were not for them, I would still be wandering along a path to nowhere. From personal cultivation to validating Dafa, I am grateful for all the help and encouragement from my fellow practitioners. I am also grateful for the teaching and numerous enlightenment opportunities provided by Master Li. Only with all this help and support am I able to improve step by step.

Most of my friends think that this choice of mine is rather foolish; they even feel sorry for me. For someone who has not experienced cultivation firsthand, I can understand their confusion, but when a person's heart is filled with concern for others, when a person's heart is filled with kindness and justice, when a person's heart is filled with the truth of the universe, then personal gain becomes insignificant. Nothing can cause a cultivator's firm belief in the universal principles and truth to waver.

Dafa Is Rapidly Changing People's Hearts

By a practitioner in China

When I first began working at a new company, a co-worker came over to tell me about all her grievances. She did that almost every day. At first I felt it was a bit annoying, but I realized since I was cultivating Truthfulness, Compassion, and Forbearance, I should show my compassion. Therefore, I always listened patiently to her complaints, and after she was finished talking, I would tell her principles from the teachings of Falun Dafa that were applicable to her case. After that, she said that Falun Gong truly made sense, that it resolved the puzzling questions in her mind and enabled her to see things more clearly. I encouraged her to begin practicing, but she always used being "too busy" as an excuse.

Once, my co-worker was careless in her speech and offended a colleague. This colleague reported the problem to the company manager and the whole thing became more serious. I turned to *Zhuan Falun* and used the teachings to guide her. That night, she received a call from the offended colleague, who screamed at her over the phone. At once, she recalled Dafa's principles about taking matters of individual gain and interpersonal conflicts more lightly. As a result, she apologized to her colleague. The caller's attitude changed immediately, and she admitted that she herself was also at fault. The next day my co-worker told me the story, and said that she wanted to practice Dafa with me.

I had not expected that after knowing me for just a few months, she would be influenced by Dafa and elevate her character. She became much more relaxed and open-minded. Other colleagues also noticed the changes in her and told me about it, saying that Falun Dafa was truly wonderful. They said it was indeed a good cultivation practice, benefiting people in both body and mind. I knew that this was all the power of Dafa, that it could change people's hearts so rapidly.

Reading Zhuan Falun Reunited My Family

By a practitioner in China

Zhuan Falun transformed my family life. Before I began practicing Falun Dafa, my family would quarrel incessantly. Since studying *Zhuan Falun*, my family relationships have improved. After finishing *Zhuan Falun* for the first time, I began studying it regularly, doing the exercises with my classmates, and cultivating steadily in my daily life. To my surprise, I found myself changing. I stopped competing with others and began to think from other people's perspective. If there was something that others did not want to do but should be done, I would take the initiative and do it myself. At the time, my father was having an extramarital affair. He also had a bad temper and would fight with my mother. His heart was not in our home. Since I knew *Zhuan Falun* was a good book, I introduced it to my mother. Then, a miracle happened. After my mother read this book, my parents, who were divorced at the time, gradually started to get along. They went to the south to work together. Now they are living together again as a happy couple. My mother said that soon, when their business stabilizes, they will send for me!

My family and I had been shrouded in darkness. After

reading *Zhuan Falun*, my family has gone through a transformation process. Now I am enjoying the love of both parents. My family is very peaceful and harmonious. I feel so fortunate and so happy!

Living a New Life

By a Western practitioner in New Jersey, U.S.A.

I want to share with you the profound changes I've experienced in my life since beginning to practice Falun Dafa a little over a year ago. The differences are like night and day. In order for you to appreciate these differences, I must share a little about my life from the time I was a child all the way up until I started to practice.

When I was only four years old, my parents divorced. With my younger brother and mother, I moved around a lot, went to many different schools and wound up spending most of my time with older kids who introduced me to many negative things. From a very early age, drugs and sex were a driving force in my life. These elements determined everything in my life, dictating my thoughts and actions. I eventually quit school at the age of 15 because I was consumed with this demonic nature. I was good-natured at the core, but my lifestyle with drugs and women not only hurt me but also affected others, especially women.

Somewhat miraculously, despite my clouded state I was always able to hold down a decent paying job ever since I dropped out of school. I was also able to marry at the age of 19 and hold the marriage together until now, 24 years later.

During this time I raised two healthy daughters, both of whom thrive in school. Because of an innate goodness I was able to instill in my children a sense of morality and provide them with a stable environment. All the while, however, to support my bad side I always had a second job that went solely to my addictions. But no matter how they consumed me, they were unable to destroy my divine nature and my longing to cultivate.

One day my mother told me about a qigong practice called Falun Gong. In the past, there were many things that my mother had tried to introduce me to so that I could break free from my bad habits, but this was somehow different. The moment she told me about Falun Gong, I felt a subtle but powerful spark from within. I didn't want her to push anything on me, so I kept that feeling to myself. Nonetheless, the very next day she brought over Master Li's exercise video and took me through some of the exercises. Something clicked and shined like gold, but again, I kept it to myself.

I called my mom and asked her about the Falun Gong practice site in my area. I told her I wanted to go to the next one. She told me the time and location and I planned to go, but on the way to the practice site I got lost and ended up being an hour late. But for whatever reasons, the class didn't start on time. They too were an hour late. I was very pleased and apologized for being late. As we practiced the exercises that day, I felt very strong energy sensations throughout my whole body. I was amazed. I took home from the practice site the exercise videotape and the book, Falun Gong. I learned the exercises the next day and began reading the book. I exercised and studied each day until the next group practice, a week later.

That week my thoughts became clearer and clearer until a miraculous thing occurred. At the time, I had no thoughts or desires for Falun Gong to remove my addictions. In fact, I wasn't even trying to quit the drugs, alcohol, and womanizing at that point in my life. I had tried numerous times before to break those habits, but on more than one occasion I wound up in the hospital because of overwhelming withdrawal symptoms and physical shutdown. But as I practiced and studied the Fa that week, I realized that I wanted clarity. I realized that I wanted to practice and study more and that these negative things were getting in the way. That week I did fewer and fewer negative things, until the morning of the next group practice when I came to the realization that I didn't want to do those things at all. More than anything, I wanted to go to that next class clean. I threw out my drugs and alcohol and from that day since, I have never gone back. What is even more miraculous is that I didn't encounter any degree of cravings or a desire to go back to that way of life. My life was utterly changed, so quickly, so naturally. My family and friends were completely amazed. Thank you so much, Master Li.

So many profound changes have come over me in a little over one year's time. I now have a new understanding about life. The purpose of life is for me to return to my original, true self and ascend from my previous life of delusion. My only desires now are to be Truthful and Compassionate and to always Forbear. I never lose my temper and always consider others when I speak. Now that I have found Dafa, my wife and daughters always smile, as do the rest of my family and friends.

My Life Is a Lot Better When My Heart Is Practicing Truthfulness, Compassion, and Forbearance

By Augusto Andrade, Raleigh, North Carolina, U.S.A.

I live in North Carolina now, but I'm originally from Ecuador, South America.

In order to improve my spiritual life, I had been practicing some other cultivation ways for about 24 years. I had always been trying to improve the health of my body, mind and spirit. But for many years, no matter how I tried to improve the quality of my life, I always had a lot of tribulations, problems, misfortunes and miseries.

Fortunately one morning in September 1998, while walking around a lake, I saw a young man performing his meditation practice. I felt that I would like to practice that type of meditation together with him. Something stronger than my own wish was pushing me to talk with him, but I couldn't because I felt respect for what he was doing and didn't want to interrupt him. The next day, the same thing happened. But on the third day I couldn't hold my strong desire any longer, and I decided to interrupt his exercise practice. I introduced myself to him.

After a short, friendly conversation, I asked him if there were books describing his exercises. Soon afterwards he gave me a set of books: *Falun Gong, Zhuan Falun* and an exercise instruction tape. Since that day, thanks to Master Li's wonderful teachings of cultivation, and the principles of Truthfulness, Compassion, and Forbearance, my life has changed a great deal, in terms of my physical body, as well as my mind and my spirituality.

At present, I am an understanding person, and I offer my benevolence when I am mistreated in life. When I am faced with conflicts, I think this is an opportunity to increase my forbearance, and to practice what I have learned from Falun Dafa.

For example, a few weeks ago, I was returning home from group practice in the park. I was driving on a road where two lanes merged into one, and I had the right of way. Suddenly a car from the other lane cut me off. Since I was comfortably driving under the speed limit, I had no problem controlling my car. Unfortunately another person tried to do the same, but he failed, and my car was hit on the rear right side. I reduced my speed to stop. This person was so upset that he hit the back of my car again on purpose.

Both of us stepped out of our cars. As I was approaching him, he insulted me with a lot of bad words like a typical bully. At that moment I started to experience the reaction I had in a similar situation years ago, but this time my mind was thinking about Master Li's teachings on Forbearance. Therefore, with a kind voice I told this person, "I do not understand why you're so upset. It is my car which was damaged, not yours." He had no option but to calm down. When I was getting a piece of paper to write down his name and driver's license, he suddenly drove away so fast that I could not even see his license plate number.

I was thankful that, due to learning about Forbearance from Master Li, I behaved in a different way from how I used to. I did not lose anything other than a few minutes and some scratches on my car. But at the same time, I gained a lot of peace in my soul. I now know that it is indeed possible to love and forgive those who try to do bad things to us. I have experienced first-hand that my life is a lot better when my heart is practicing Truthfulness, Compassion and Forbearance.

Spiritually, I had been very dedicated to my beliefs, always hoping to get something better for my spirit, but my improvement had been very slow. In my first month of Falun Dafa practice, my character improved much faster compared with my previous 24 years in other spiritual practices. Today I have more control over my thoughts, and through the exercises I can drain out the negative thoughts that enter my mind. Before, it was almost impossible to do so.

Increasing my Forbearance in conjunction with Truthfulness and Compassion is a great blessing that is enlightening my life, which allows me to share the peace that everybody wants to feel inside. Because of the above changes, today I am a peaceful, harmonious, healthy, and happy person, with a lot more tenderness, benevolence, love, respect, tolerance, understanding and forgiveness, not only for my family members, but for all of humanity.

In short, I think Falun Dafa is great. I hope, from the bottom of my heart, that every single person in the world will get the opportunity to learn about Falun Dafa.

I Found Falun Dafa and
Left Behind My Life of Crime

By a practitioner in China

Had I not found Master Li's Falun Dafa, I would not still be in this world. I used to go astray routinely and became involved in crime. I pursued money and material pleasure. I dared to do any bad thing and eventually descended into the hell of drug addiction. I tried to quit, but without the desire to be good from within my heart, abstinence was impossible. I spent all of my savings on drugs. In order to obtain money for more drugs, I participated in mob plots and was beaten. My right hand was broken and a crashing fall fractured both my feet. My wife left me, there was nothing left in my house, I became emaciated, and yet the bad habits still ensnared me. I thought I had come to the end of my life and prepared to leave this world by committing suicide.

Before killing myself, I went to say farewell to my only friend. Fortunately, he was practicing Falun Dafa at the time and recommended it to me. I opened *Zhuan Falun* and read the preface and the first lecture. I immediately knew *Zhuan Falun* was not an ordinary book. I eagerly read it through and totally forgot about my suicidal thoughts.

I decided to cultivate and took the first step on the path to start my life over again. Through learning the Fa, I understood that the real purpose of life is to return to one's original, true self by cultivating and assimilating to the nature of the universe, *Zhen* (Truthfulness), *Shan* (Compassion), *Ren* (Forbearance). Through cultivation practice I would discard all of my bad habits.

The first thing was to abstain from drugs. Addiction specialists were astounded when I quit taking drugs without taking any medication the second day after I read *Zhuan Falun*. Restricting myself to the cosmic characteristic of Truthfulness-Compassion-Forbearance, I firmly practiced Falun Dafa and have never used drugs again. Some former addict companions came to my house and wanted to do drugs, but they could not rekindle my old desire, and I even advised them to quit. They never bothered me again. I let go of my past life completely.

Now, I have a legitimate profession, a fulfilling life, and a healthy body. I am full of energy. Master Li and Falun Gong saved me and provided me with a bright path of life.

Practicing Falun Dafa in the Taiwanese Army

By Hao Bai, Kao-hsiong, Taiwan

I became a Falun Dafa practitioner in May 2003. Although I knew at that time that Falun Dafa was very good, I didn't participate in the 9-day lecture class or the local practice for various reasons. But at some point, I decided to study Dafa seriously, even though I was extremely busy writing my thesis for a Master's degree. I studied the Fa and Master Li's other lectures at a certain time each day. Gradually I developed a deeper understanding of the Fa and its profoundness.

Six months later when I got my degree, I had to face another test—joining the army. According to the law in Taiwan, all adult young men, unless they have specific physical or psychological problems, have to serve in the army. Daily life in the training center for new recruits was filled with intense drills. I was not allowed to do the Falun Gong exercises. We were not even allowed to talk to each other most of the time. I told myself that if I could not do the exercises, I would focus on cultivating my character. There were so many things to endure in the army. At critical moments, I always remembered Master Li's words that we are cultivators. We should be kind to other people while holding ourselves to a high standard. Every day I would either read *Zhuan Falun* or talk to my classmates about Falun Gong for half an hour before going to bed. To those who could accept what I said and showed an interest in Falun Gong, I would lend them *Zhuan Falun* or give them the book.

After two months of preliminary training and three months of special training, I was appointed captain of a troop of coastal patrols. My responsibility was to command the troops and take care of the soldiers. Since there was not a deputy captain in my unit, I had to assume that position as well. In addition, I was appointed to the catering committee. At the same time, I was the only Officer on Duty in the unit, and I was busy every day. Although as a captain I had my own small room, I rarely had more than ten minutes of private time before someone knocked on the door and said, "Captain, so-and-so is looking for you." Most of my time was thus consumed. But I just held to one point: cultivating my character.

I kept on reminding myself that Master Li wanted me to be a good person in every aspect, so I did daily work with the soldiers. Whenever I had some time, I would talk to the officers and soldiers, trying to learn their family situations, if they felt O.K. in the army, and if they had any difficulties. I tried my best to help them solve their problems. At the same time, I took the opportunity to introduce Falun Dafa and tell them about the persecution of Falun Dafa by the Chinese Communist Party.

Since the soldiers were very young, slightly over 20, or

only teenagers, it was easy for them to understand when I talked about the persecution and human rights abuses. Yet it was not easy to introduce Dafa to them. They often thought that Buddha and gods were something abstract that only existed in legends.

I only gave the book *Zhuan Falun* to a few soldiers who had a strong interest and were quite receptive to Dafa, so they had a chance to understand the profoundness of Dafa by themselves. As for other people, I chose to talk about the miraculous effects of Falun Gong in eliminating illnesses. They liked to hear stories about that. Every time I told them my own experience, they looked amazed, but they could accept it. Some started to ask questions about Falun Gong. I tried my best to tell them what was said in *Zhuan Falun*. Some started to introduce Falun Gong to their families. When a soldier was depressed or felt wronged and upset, I made time to offer comfort and help with the situation. Depending on the occasion, I would tell him about the principles of Falun Dafa to let him know that there was a reason for everything.

I am grateful to be able to spread Dafa in the army. I realize that as Dafa practitioners, our every word certainly will have an impact on people in society and their views on Dafa and Dafa practitioners. Cultivating character at all times, treating everyone kindly in our lives, and watching our words, thoughts, and actions is the best way to clarify the truth and validate the Fa. It is natural and peaceful, reaching deep into the heart. It is also a way to spread the great benevolence Master Li has imparted to us.

Two months before I left the army, I was appointed as a Counseling Officer, and I did not have to take care of so much routine business every day. I had more time. If nothing special happened, I would do the four standing exercises during the lunch break and the meditation before going to bed. My supervisor gave orders to move the counseling office to a bigger room and asked me to decorate it myself. Seeing that there was a blank wall right behind the desk and the paint on the wall had peeled off, I went to the Yiqun Bookstore in Taipei on a holiday and bought a big poster with the words "Falun Dafa is good." I put it on the wall where the paint had peeled off. People who came into the room, before speaking to me, would look at the poster and read aloud, "Falun Dafa is good." Then they asked, "What indeed is Falun Dafa?" I would take the opportunity to clarify the truth to them. As a result, almost everyone in my troop learned about Dafa and knew that Falun Dafa is good.

One night in December, at around 10 o'clock, a soldier who was about to leave the army came into the counseling room. He said directly to me, "Captain, I often heard you mention Falun Gong, but I had no time to ask you about it. What indeed is Falun Gong? Is it really so miraculous? How is it different from Buddhism?" I gave him a brief explanation and handed him the book *Zhuan Falun*. He was very happy and said, "I will read it right away."

At 12:30 a.m., someone ran into my room without knocking. It was him. He looked a little shocked. He came in, threw himself in the chair, and said, "Captain, I have never encountered anything so spectacular."

The next day, he finished reading the whole book. Although both of us were about to leave the army, we seized the time to do the exercises in the Counseling Room during the noon break. Later the medical officer joined us, too, until we left the army in January of that year.

Falun Dafa Turned My Life Around

By Caylan Ford, Calgary, Canada

When I was a young child, I would often contemplate the meaning of life. I always sought to get closer to nature so as to understand the underlying reasons and order of things in the universe. I knew, as most everyone must, that there was something more to life than what was being presented to me. Perhaps it was childish self-centeredness, or maybe it wasn't, but I always felt that destiny had great things in store for me.

As I got a little older and became more familiar with the workings of this secular society, I grew increasingly pessimistic and fearful that I would never discover the true purpose of my life. This prospect haunted me day in and day out, eventually causing me so much anxiety that it even became difficult to breathe. By the time I was 11, I had grown very bitter towards the world and the apparent meaninglessness of life, and my health began to deteriorate. By age 13, I had started drinking excessively and doing and selling drugs. My lifestyle led me to adopt many warped notions; I fully subscribed to communist theories, and even read communist literature. I was also staunchly opposed to traditional morality, particularly towards upright religions, and eventually I stopped believing in right and wrong altogether.

Shortly after turning 14, I was kicked out of my house. By that time I was starting to have pancreas problems from drinking too much. I couldn't make it through the day without a drink, and was almost a completely dysfunctional human being. My mind had become so complex and full of chaotic notions that I couldn't sit through a whole day of school or stay awake through class. Even the simplest tasks had become nearly impossible.

At that time, I knew I had to change the direction of my life. I began devoting myself more to spiritual pursuits. Though I was extremely foggy-headed, I came to understand that I must find a way to achieve internal freedom, let go of my notions, and live in harmony with the universe. The problem was, I had no idea how to work towards this goal. Throughout my life I had been exposed to a number of new age theories and religious philosophies, but none of them struck me as being very profound or genuine.

Even though I had started to put my life back in order, I still lived with a near constant worry that I would never discover the meaning of this life. I was still plagued by health problems, including some lingering effects of the drugs I did when I was younger. My relationships with my family were generally poor (I barely spoke with my father for years), and I did countless degenerate things, some of which are even painful to remember.

It was at that time, when I was 15 years old, that a friend introduced me to Falun Gong.

I can still vividly remember the first night I started

reading *Zhuan Falun*. I was in a very bitter mood, and was also feeling quite angry and jealous. Since I had nothing else to do, I picked up *Zhuan Falun* and read the first lecture. The principles contained within it struck a deep chord with me. Even though much of the vocabulary was over my head, there was something familiar and comforting about the book. By the time I was done, I had a remarkable sensation that I had never experienced before. It was a sense of true calm, of contentment from the bottom of my heart. The jealousy and bitterness that only hours before had seemed to consume me had disappeared. That night, I went to sleep smiling, and got the best sleep of my life. A part of me understood that I no longer needed to fear never finding the meaning of life. I felt like my long wait was finally over. I had finally come home.

When I finally decided to commit myself to the path of Dafa cultivation, I started to experience many of the things described in *Zhuan Falun*. My illnesses all disappeared in a very short period of time. Within about a week of becoming determined to be a Dafa disciple and learning the exercises, I was involved in a car accident. An SUV slammed into the car door that I was sitting next to, crushing the door and shattering the glass. At that time, I was not worried or hurt. After I began practicing Dafa, old friends would always comment that I looked much younger (how much younger could I get?), and that my face looked so much more radiant.

My relationships with my family were also finally mended. In particular, my relationship with my father had a turning point the first time I told him about Falun Gong. Although he's a very serious man with no spiritual or religious beliefs, he had an unexplainable and immediate affinity towards Falun Gong. Having seen the dramatic changes in my character, he became very supportive of Dafa. He even supported me in my Dafa work (financially) and sometimes helped pay for trips to conferences. My mother also took an immediate liking to Falun Gong, and both of them often talk to their friends about the persecution in China.

The next year, I graduated from high school one year early and at the top of my class. In the span of a little over two years, the changes in my life were dramatic. I had gone from nearly dropping out of school, being distant and cold towards my family, drinking almost every day, indulging in countless degenerate activities, and being self-centered and jealous, to being a Dafa practitioner whose entire being had been renewed from the deepest source.

Turning Difficulties Into Opportunities to Cultivate Truthfulness, Compassion, and Forbearance

By a Western practitioner in the U.S.A.

Like many Westerners, I've had a long term interest in Eastern philosophies and holistic practices, including acupuncture, Chinese herbal medicine, Tai Chi, qigong, and the mind/body connection. I wanted to understand the purpose of life, to live in harmony with nature, and to have a long and healthy life. I think that the ancient culture of China, with all its wisdom and knowledge, has a lot to teach us about how to live in harmony with nature and with each other.

I feel that Falun Gong is the crown jewel of the traditional culture of China. Oriental medicine teaches that to have a long and healthy life, "You have to have a clean heart and few desires." Falun Gong teaches us how to have a clean heart and few desires. It's not about looking for external solutions to one's problems or illnesses. It's about goodness, about cultivating our character.

I've practiced for a little more than three years and I've experienced profound changes in my outlook, understanding, and health. I teach in the difficult environment of a public high school where it's easy to become judgmental and impatient with students. Falun Gong practice helps me stay balanced and calm and to turn the difficulties into opportunities to cultivate Truthfulness, Compassion, Forbearance, the core principles of Falun Gong. Our children, our schools, and every aspect of society would be greatly improved if we restored these principles to their proper place in our hearts.

A New Life for My Family and Me

By Nina Akbar, Hamburg, Germany

I am 26-years-old and learned about Falun Dafa more than a year ago from my sister's classmate. At that time I was very critical of Dafa. It took another good three months before I decided to give it a try. I simply could not get it out of my mind.

Perhaps I could not believe that something as good as Dafa had come my way. During my search for the meaning of life and for the origin of life I encountered many negative experiences. It seemed too simplistic to me that one could return to the truth and the origin merely with the aid of a book and five cultivation exercises.

Even as a small child I enjoyed going out by myself in the evening. I would sit all by myself in the dark and sense a longing and ache in my heart. I wanted to go somewhere, but did not know the way. The world seemed shallow and full of contradictions. But yet, deep down inside of me I always knew what was right and what was wrong, but how it played out was different. On one hand I always desired to be diligent, polite and unassuming. I didn't want to stand out and had not much desire for material things. On the other hand, I always compared myself to others. What they had,

I also wanted. What they knew how to do, I also wanted to be able to accomplish. So I began to aspire to go after personal advantages and recognition. In school I wanted to be the best, but somehow that was not enough anymore. I also wanted many friends and to be popular. Then, that was no longer enough. I wanted excitement, wanted to collect experiences and to become worldly wise and travel. I lived in constant restlessness, unsatisfied with myself, and was not able to handle my lot in life. In the beginning, my family and friends worried about me and about my future, but then many of them gave up and we lost contact.

Since I have found Dafa, the restlessness and uncertainty no longer plague me. I have become stable and feel more balanced. I am presently studying to become a teacher, to teach special education students. This is something important for me, because I can see a purpose in it. I see my tasks in this world and am firmly committed to go my way, and have nothing interfere with my cultivation or deter me from it. I found that which gives me strength to handle my feelings and tribulations and has answered all my questions. I no longer feel sorry for myself when I encounter a difficulty, nor do I need to run away from my problems. I now know how to handle problems and also know that the problems that I encounter are a way for me to pay back some of my karmic debts. All of a sudden, things have become light, simple and natural.

I no longer have to chase after good fortune, health, love or knowledge. Everything I need to become happy, to reach the ultimate state, is in the book *Zhuan Falun*. Everything that is destined to come into my life will come. I don't have to pursue anything. Everything will come by itself.

I am busy with my studies. I don't always take the easy road, but study what is pertinent and interesting and what seems to be important. I want to do a good job because doing it this way I found out makes me more content. I am also no longer as impatient as before. My thoughts are not preoccupied with wanting to have my own way when I have to complete a joint task. It turns out that I don't have to sacrifice my own ideas. It so happens that I always get a chance to include my own ideas. I am in a much better position to listen to others and achieve harmonious cooperation. I can almost feel how Compassion and Forbearance are taking root my heart.

Thanks to Falun Dafa, my family situation has also changed for the better. Before I obtained Dafa, my sister, brother, and parents all lived in different parts of the city. Except for my sister and I, the rest of the family seldom met in a family circle. Somehow, everyone lived their own lives. Part of the reason for that was the problematic relationship with my father. We simply could not communicate. Routinely the visits would end in a verbal battle. My father would no longer acknowledge me as his daughter and would throw me out of the house. I could not take that and avoided him. Strangely enough, my siblings did not have these problems with him. Since I could not resolve this problem, I chalked up his angry outbursts to the mental illness from which he suffered and in the process of this reasoning brought the rest of the family over to my side, so that I could assert my own will anytime I needed something.

Since I have practiced Falun Dafa, our relationship has totally changed. Now that I am willing to exercise forbearance in the fights with him and see those fights as a chance to improve my character, we seldom have fights anymore. For the first time I sense that I see him as the person he really is. I don't see his illness any longer. When he starts yelling at me out of the blue, it does not bother me anymore and I manage to remain calm. This allows me to see his sorrow, fear and suffering. Our relationship improved to the point where he invited me to move back in with them. At first I was reluctant to give up my freedom and was afraid to become dependent. But then I changed my mind and did move back in with my parents. It cannot be by chance that he made me this offer. I see it as a great opportunity to advance on my path of cultivation.

When I told my brother of my decision to move back home, he could understand me right away. Then he ventured on his own that it would be best if our sister would move in with him, a good solution for us, since then we would all be physically much closer to each other. It would also shorten my sister's commute to school. We were all very touched, because under no circumstances did he want to have a sister living with him before. He had highly valued his freedom and independence. In the meantime, both of us sisters moved; I to my parents' home, and my sister moved in with my brother. That was a big relief for us. My sister helps our brother with his household and both of us sisters are giving our mother a hand with the housework. We take most meals with our parents. When there is time, we do the exercises together or read. That seems to make everything easier. We are all quite happy, in spite of day-to-day squabbles. My father, for the first time in his life, seems to have blossomed and is happy to have his children back.

He is the only one among us who does not practice Falun Gong, but he allows us to practice in peace and quiet and trusts us. That alone shows me what positive results Falun Gong can have.

Thank You, Master Li

By a Japanese-American practitioner in New Jersey, U.S.A.

I'm 53 years old and have practiced Falun Dafa for about 5 months.

In spite of the goodness of my parents and six siblings, throughout my childhood, there always was a feeling of loneliness and isolation in my mind. In my young adulthood, I was very honest and someone once warned me not to be too honest; that made me feel stupid. After that I struggled to not be too honest and stupid. I gradually became "smarter" as I aged, but it was against my conscience, and the sense of isolation from my childhood was still there.

I came to the United States from Japan 30 years ago to marry my fiancé. I have been quite happy after marrying, at least in my private life. On the surface probably I looked normal, but I could not help feeling foreign among my Japanese coworkers and friends, and I had a tendency to retreat into myself and my family. After many years of striving, I started to learn how to be on my own and to follow my own conscience and judgment. I kept saying to myself, "It's ok to be different." When I was about to reach 50, like many other women of similar age, I started to have a hormone imbalance that brought chaos to my health. Many of the problems could be controlled by taking herbs, but most of the herbs were not supposed to be taken for a prolonged period. As soon as I stopped taking them the problems came back.

About the same time, I became interested in meditation and was looking for an opportunity to learn it, without success. Then one day someone introduced me to Falun Dafa. After the sitting meditation, we read the book, *Zhuan Falun*. Immediately, it fascinated me. After all those years I found a book that told me my conscience had been right. I went back to the practice site again the next week. The book was telling us about tribulations this time. I thought, "This is it. Sure, there is a purpose for our sufferings." I was delighted. The truth was that this book struck me deep in my heart without any apparent reason. And whatever the reason was, I knew I had found something which I had almost given up searching for. A month later, I attended a nine-day seminar. When about two months had passed, I suddenly realized that I hadn't taken any herbs for a long time and I was feeling fine.

When I became serious about cultivation, my desire for making Falun Dafa known to other people grew. I started to participate in activities whenever possible with a fear deep in my mind, the fear that I would be forced to face my greatest weakness and change it; that is, my unusual shyness and nervousness. I have lived all my life avoiding the spotlight. The thought of talking to strangers made me nervous. Master Li has said that fear is an attachment. It was unavoidable to go through this ordeal to remove that attachment.

As the persecution in China kept getting worse, I joined other practitioners at the mall to collect signatures for a petition and to raise awareness of the persecution in China. At first I did not know how to talk to the people and I was at a loss. As a result I was not very successful in getting the signatures. With remorse, I took a moment at home trying to think what was wrong with me.

Soon another trial was given to me. I was to go to the community center on Martin Luther King Jr.'s birthday. There was a large assembly going on, and with another practitioner I was supposed to collect signatures for the same petition. Since my fellow practitioner had no experience, I was nervous again. But when the assembly was over and people came out one by one, without thinking much, the words came out of my mouth naturally. I felt my attachment become smaller.

In the past months, I have been forced to face my weaknesses and defects one by one. The tests never seem to cease coming.

Once I was supposed to do a job for someone and forgot about it. When that person called me to see if the job was done, I said, "Sure, it's ready," and as soon as I hung up I started to do the job. I did the job but I had a very uncomfortable feeling in my mind. I said to myself, "Was this a lie? Yes, I think it was. But it did not harm anyone, why is it bothering me? That's because it is against the law of the universe." Soon after, on a different matter I lied again and this time I immediately regretted it and thought about why I did it. It became apparent that I lied to make myself look more capable and better than I actually was. It was an attachment of pride. I felt ashamed. When a third trial came, I told the truth and apologized.

Now, Falun Dafa has become a part of my life. Where has the loneliness in my heart gone? I cannot find it anywhere. Thank you, Master Li.

Epilogue : A Few Words from the Editors

As editors of this book and practitioners of Falun Dafa, we sincerely hope that you have found the reading enjoyable and informative. Although not everyone experiences the remarkable benefits the contributors to this book have described, we have all gained genuine improvement in character from practicing Falun Dafa. Through living according to the principles of Truthfulness, Compassion, and Forbearance, we have discovered a state of being that we previously did not imagine possible. In the hope that even more people can benefit from this wonderful practice, we would like to invite you to try out Falun Dafa for yourself.

Resources:

·   All of the Falun Dafa teachings can be downloaded free of charge at http://falundafa.org/. Many of the books can also be purchased at local bookstores, or ordered online at www.truegoodbooks.com. You may learn the five simple-to-do exercises by watching the videos online, contacting a practitioner near you (see http://falundafa.org/eng/local. htm), or simply by asking any practitioner that you run into at one of our events.

· This book's companion volume, *Life and Hope Renewed --The Healing Power of Falun Dafa*, can be downloaded at http://www.clearwisdom.net/emh/136/

· To read more articles by Falun Dafa practitioners such as those found in this book, as well as news of the persecution in China and practitioners' activities around the world, visit the Clearwisdom.net website at www.clearwisdom.net.

Glossary

610 Office : an agency specifically created to persecute Falun Gong, with absolute power over each level of administration in the Party and all other political and judiciary systems.

"April 25" : This refers to April 25, 1999, when ten thousand Falun Gong practitioners peacefully gathered at the State Council's Appeals Bureau in Beijing near the government compound at Zhongnanhai and successfully appealed for the release of forty-five practitioners who had been unjustly arrested in Tianjin City.

Clarifying the Truth : Because of the persecution in China and the unrelenting hate campaign carried out by China's state-controlled media, Falun Gong practitioners have been actively "clarifying the truth" by explaining to the public the facts about Falun Gong and exposing the persecution. Truth clarification activities include face-to-face conversations with people, posting notices and posters, handing out flyers, and hanging banners. Outside of China, where Falun Gong is freely practiced, practitioners further expose the persecution through anti-torture reenactments, art exhibits, Internet websites, books, magazines, newspapers, movies and letter writing. The goal of clarifying the truth is to help people understand Falun Gong, to dispel the lies of the communist regime in China and to raise public support to end the persecution. (Variation: "clarifying the facts")

Cultural Revolution : A communist political movement that denounced traditional values and culture (1966-1976)

Dafa : "Great Law;" principles

Fa : Law and principles; the teachings of Falun Dafa.

Gong : 1. cultivation energy; 2. practice that cultivates such energy

Nine Commentaries on the Communist Party : *A* book published in late 2004 that reveals the true nature of the Communist Party. The *Nine Commentaries* have led millions of people to renounce their membership in the Chinese Communist Party (CCP) and its affiliated organizations. http://ninecommentaries.com

Qigong : A form of traditional Chinese practice which cultivates qi or "vital energy."

Ren : Forbearance, Endurance, Tolerance